TEMPORAL
DELUSION

T. A. MCMAHON

Co-author of THE SEDUCTION OF CHRISTIANITY

BEND • OREGON

TEMPORAL DELUSION

Published by The Berean Call
Copyright ©2013

ISBN 978-1-928660-71-2

Unless otherwise indicated, Scripture quotations are from
The Holy Bible, King James Version (KJV)

COPYRIGHT & FAIR USE

The Berean Call
PO Box 7019
Bend, Oregon, 97708-7020

PRINTED IN THE UNITED STATES OF AMERICA

CONTENTS

INTRODUCTION

The *TBC* articles that we have selected for this book all relate to a development that the Bible indicates will take place in the latter days just prior to the Second Coming of Jesus Christ. At that time, a religion led by the Antichrist will win the hearts and minds of nearly all who populate the earth. This will follow an event known as the Rapture, in which Christ will return to take all true believers to Heaven.

Almost all of the earth's remaining population will be compelled to follow the Antichrist and submit to his religion, which will not just suddenly appear without precedent; rather, it will be an accumulation of what has been in process since the Fall of mankind in the Garden of Eden, false teachings added upon false teachings, century after century. Those cumulative corruptions and distortions of biblical truth will accommodate all spiritual beliefs, yet this resulting worldwide religion will maintain a superficial veneer of Christianity.

Ecumenism, originally the promotion of unity among churches and denominations that profess to be Christian, has now been extended to include all "people of faith." It is presently playing a major part in the end times dilution of Christianity, and it is enticing both professing and true Christians. Scripture tells us that in the Last Days prior to the Rapture, many Christians will "not endure sound doctrine"; that is, they will be seduced away from the Word of God.

Without that light of truth to guide their path, they will be vulnerable to every wind of doctrine.

One such deception is the subject of this book; it is a *temporal* delusion that consists of diverting Christians away from the teaching of Scripture regarding the Kingdom of God. The Bible tells us that Christ's Kingdom will be literally established at His Second Coming. At that time, He will return from Heaven to this earth, which will have undergone the cataclysmic devastation that God will have poured out in His wrath against the Antichrist and all those who have followed him. Christ's purpose will be to rescue Israel from the annihilation intended by the world and its leader and to begin His Millennial reign upon the earth.

Eschatology (beliefs related to the last days) has rarely been an essential part of the theology of most Christians because they have regarded it as too far in the future to have any consequence in their daily lives. Those times have changed drastically.

The temporal delusion is upon us and comprises teachings, concepts, practices, programs, beliefs, agendas, etc., that deviate from the biblical doctrine of the Second Coming. Nearly all, in one aspect or another, teach that the Kingdom must be established prior to the physical return of Christ. All of them disparage the prophetic teachings of the Bible that do not confirm their various "reclaim or fix the earth for Christ" agendas. The included "good works" that attend such efforts make the process incredibly seductive, even to many true believers who lack the discernment to recognize the perversion of the Scripture involved.

As Dave Hunt has noted in *Whatever Happened to Heaven?*, those who believe they are working for the Kingdom of God by attempting to build His Kingdom prior to His return, no matter how sincere, will be unwittingly working to establish the kingdom of the Antichrist. When asked about the Last Days by His disciples, Jesus characterized those critical days by responding with this warning: "Take heed that no man deceive you."

It is our prayer that the following articles will inform our readers concerning the unbiblical developments in Christendom that have weaned many believers away from the Scriptures. We also pray that what we've written will encourage the body of Christ to be all the more discerning as the times become more spiritually deceptive.

T. A. McMahon

1

WEANING EVANGELICALS OFF THE WORD

Sanctify them through thy truth: thy word is truth.

—JOHN 17:17—

Apostasy is rampant within the evangelical church today. At least that's my perspective as one who has observed religious trends and developments for three decades. Before I present my specific concerns, let me define some terms. The use of the word "evangelical" in this article simply refers to those who would say that the Bible is their authority in all matters of faith and practice. "Apostasy" consists of those teachings and practices that are contrary to the Word of God yet seduce and deceive both professing Christians and true believers. "*Biblical* apostasy" is a falling away that will result in a false Christianity under the control of the Antichrist: "Let no man deceive you by any means: for that day shall not come, except there come a falling away..."(2 Thessalonians 2:3). Although the culmination of the Apostasy takes place after the Rapture of the church, various aspects of this apostate religion have and will continue to ensnare many believers throughout its development.

At a certain point in the future, there will be a total rejection of biblical Christianity, succeeded by the religion of the Antichrist; it will maintain a *veneer* of Christianity that will prove acceptable to all religions. This perversion of Christianity doesn't just suddenly happen once the Antichrist appears. The deception process began long ago in the Garden of Eden with Satan's seduction of Eve, and it is becoming more and more of a corrupting influence within Christianity as the time of the appearing of the false messiah, whom the entire world will worship (Revelation 13), draws near.

Satan began his dialogue with Eve by planting seeds of doubt regarding what God had commanded: "Yea, hath God said...?" (Genesis 3:1). This opening line of the Adversary has been the basis ever since for his principal strategy in inducing rebellion against God. Its implications impugning the character of God and sanctioning the rationalizations of man seem endless: Why would God keep something good from you?; Is He *really* in charge?; Does *He* make the rules?; You misunderstood His commands; There are no absolutes; You need to consider what He says from your own perspective, and so forth. Eve, although reiterating God's command for the most part, adds her own erroneous thought to what God actually said: "...neither shall ye touch it" (3:3).

This is what happens when dialogues take place regarding absolutes: the truth is either added to or subtracted from. Tragically, many Christians see nothing wrong with rewriting God's Word. They are perfectly content with Bible versions that have done exactly that.

In response to Eve, Satan blatantly rejects God's warning that death would result from sin: "You will *not* surely die." Making God out to be a liar or dismissing Him altogether has always been Satan's game. The Serpent then convinces Eve that obeying God's command would rob her of enlightenment, godhood, and knowledge—and thus severely limit her potential: "For God doth know that in the day ye eat thereof, then your eyes shall be opened, and ye shall be as gods, knowing good and evil" (3:5).

Variations of these basic lies from the one who was a liar from the beginning (John 8:44) have successfully deceived humanity throughout history. "Yea, hath God said...?" (Satan's direct attack upon God's Word) has even led both professing and true Christians into the Apostasy.

Questioning or rejecting what God has said in the Scriptures is at the heart of instigating religious rebellion. The reasons should be obvious: 1) If the Bible cannot be trusted as God's specific communication to mankind, then we are left with nothing more than man's opinions and guesses about God and what He desires; 2) Finite humanity's speculations about its infinite Creator are not only terribly erroneous—they are evil, because they are generated by man's sinful, self-serving nature; 3) Even a true believer could be led into darkness without the light and lamp of God's Word (Psalm 119:105).

Although the Bible has been under various attacks for centuries, the latest "Yea, hath God said...?" strategy may be the Serpent of Old's most deadly. The process involves weaning evangelical Christians away from the knowledge of, an understanding of, and a dependence upon the Word of God. The objective is to produce biblically shallow Christians who are *functionally illiterate* regarding what the Bible teaches, and who therefore have no accurate basis for, or interest in, discerning biblical truth from error. By "functionally illiterate" I mean that such evangelicals know how to read, and they have Bibles (of some sort), but they rarely read them, preferring to get their biblical content from some other source.

Conditioned by a subversive weaning process, these biblically shallow Christians have little or no concern about doctrine. They major in the *experiential*, with their feelings almost exclusively determining what they believe. The Apostle Paul, speaking prophetically of the Last Days, seemed to have these specifically in mind: "For the time will come when they will not endure sound doctrine; but after their own lusts shall they heap to themselves teachers, having itching ears; and they shall turn away their ears from the truth, and shall be turned unto fables" (2 Timothy 4:3,4). Sensual "lusts" of the flesh and imagination are implied here.

A couple of decades ago, the extreme Charismatics and Pentecostals would have been the obvious reference point regarding Paul's warning, given their obsession with healing, prosperity, and a spirituality energized by seeking after signs and wonders. Today, experiential Christianity has extended far beyond the bounds of what was considered a fringe evangelical element. It now pervades the entire church, including those denominations and movements once known for their conservative doctrinal views and biblical adherence. They have vigorously blocked the lying signs and wonders seduction at

city of
Dabiq in Syria
near ~~Alle~~ Aleppo.
Islams show-down w/Rome

Netanyahu P.M. (Israel)
King Abdullah II (Jordan)
el-Sisi president (Egypt)
} alliance against
IRAN + ISIS

ed, but I had to to save my
I don't know the lady, I
letters. I know nothing."
en, alone to a cell, down a
only a single light bulb
y. It was dark and when
1 by, I was made to face
t see who it was. It was
nd prison. There was a

their front doors while opening wide their side entrances and youth rooms to the purveyors of the experiential in less obvious yet equally disastrous forms.

Before examples of today's antibiblical experiential Christianity are presented, it needs to be understood that true Christianity is both *doctrinal* and *experiential.* It includes a personal relationship with Jesus Christ that begins when one has understood the doctrine (i.e., biblical teaching) of salvation—the Gospel of Christ—and has accepted it by faith. When this happens, the Spirit of Christ indwells that person (Ephesians 1:13; 4:30, Romans 8:9). As one understands all that He did for us, true love for Jesus follows.

Then, as one grows in his relationship with Jesus through knowing and obeying the Scriptures, one's affection for Him increases. Furthermore, as one matures in the faith, the fruit of the Spirit is increasingly manifested: love, joy, peace, longsuffering, gentleness, goodness, faith, meekness, and temperance. These certainly involve the experiential. So what's the problem with experiential Christianity?

The chief error today in the evangelical church is that experiences (feelings, emotions, passions, intuitions, etc.) have become the guide for entering into and attempting to establish true spirituality. Rather than subjective feelings and emotions being present as a *result* of one's adherence to sound doctrine, they have become the *judge* of whether or not something is truly Christian. Instead of testing a teaching, practice, or situation by the Word of God, the arbiter becomes "how one feels about it." This puts the human imagination in the seat of judgment. That thought alone should provoke an emotion in the heart of every Bible-believing Christian: sheer horror! Doctrinally however, it's even more frightening.

Twice in the Book of Proverbs, in almost exactly the same terms, we are told, "There is a way which seemeth right unto a man, but the end thereof are the ways of death" (Proverbs 14:12; 16:25). In other words, if a man goes by what he thinks or feels, independently of and in opposition to what God has declared, the consequences for him will only generate destruction. Death is the separation of the spirit and soul from the body; moreover, the ways of death include separating man from the light of God's truth. "To the law and to the testimony: if they speak not according to this word, it is because there is no light in them" (Isaiah 8:20).

Experientialism (what *feels* right to man) is a leaven working its way through the entire church as it undermines biblical truth. Today there are many infectious manifestations, with heavy emphasis upon the following: signs and wonders, faith-healing and prosperity, *logos* vs. *rhema*, the new apostles and prophets, kingdom-dominion, redeeming-the-culture missions, strategic spiritual warfare, inner-healing, 12-steps, Christian psychology, evangelical social-activism; ecumenism, church growth, purpose-driven, emerging church, contemplative/mysticism, church entertainment, contemporary music worship, culturally accommodating Bible versions, and visually translated Bibles. All of these movements are in opposition to the clear teaching of God's Word, yet multitudes follow them eagerly.

Although these diverse endeavors often overlap in terms of concepts and methods, they share a common trait: while giving lip service to the Scriptures, they all, whether through ignorance, self-delusion, or planned deceit, critically subvert its teachings. The way that seems right to a man—the way that *feels* right, produces numerical growth, *seems* more spiritual, moves one emotionally, appears to move God on one's behalf, brings people together, makes people *feel* closer to God and better about themselves, is more positive, fills more pews, impresses the world, is not judgmental, etc.—that way is systematically eliminating any concern for sound doctrine in the church. This is experientialism in opposition to doctrine among evangelicals, and by it, the church is helping to usher in the Apostasy.

There is not enough space to explain all the movements listed above. We have been writing about most of them for years. Many of them can be found by searching TBC's website for related articles or the books we offer. Although they are connected at times by individuals, similar methodologies, or goals, the basic glue that essentially holds all of the movements together is the propensity for subjective experience over the written Word. All are working from this same unbiblical premise.

Extreme Charismatics and Pentecostals have a foundational teaching that God's mode of communication today is to speak outside the Bible directly to His people, particularly through a new breed of apostles and prophets. This "new way" is called the *rhema* of God, a supposed contrast to *logos*, which is categorized as the old written form. One of it's foremost leaders, C. Peter Wagner, claims that God is instructing the church in new ways of doing things through His modern prophets.

The Bible, therefore, is of little or no value for judging what's being promoted. This teaching is not only antibiblical, but it has been the catalyst for the most spiritually spurious rituals of the last century, from the proliferation of false prophets to the so-called binding of territorial spirits to taking dominion over cities, countries, and, ultimately, the world—"for the Lord."

Hearing from and drawing experientially closer to God through techniques (e.g., occult visualization and meditation) is the practice of today's evangelical contemplatives and mystics. Richard Foster and others have derived their so-called spiritual formation approach from Catholic "saints" and mystics. Foster created *The Renovaré Spiritual Formation Bible* to biblically support his mystical approach, yet its commentaries libel the Scriptures and demean sound doctrine. Foster introduced Eastern mystical techniques to the church decades ago in *Celebration of Discipline* (quickly adopted as mandatory reading for Campus Crusade leadership). Now his spiritual formation agenda is foundational to the Emerging Church, a widespread movement of 20-to-30-year-old evangelicals who are attracted to the sensual liturgies (candles, incense, chanting, vestments, rituals, statues, icons, etc.) of Roman Catholicism and Eastern Orthodoxy as a supposed means of enhancing their spiritual formation.

Eugene Peterson, a contributor to *The Renovaré Bible*, has his own extremely popular Bible version, *The Message*. Experientialism through alleged poetic license is blatantly manifested throughout this humanistic and culturally acceptable perversion of God's Word, which Rick Warren has done much to promote. Consider Matthew 16:25 in *The Message*:

"Self-help is no help at all. Self-sacrifice is the way, my way, to finding yourself, your true self." Try finding any hint of one's "true self" in any other Bible translation of this verse! This is the leaven of psychotherapy (which is wholly experiential and subjective) that has permeated the church.

Although on guard against the biblical abuses of the Charismatics, even the most conservative evangelical churches have been seduced by the self-oriented and feelings-sensitive methodologies of psychology. Nothing in contemporary Christianity has raised the cry of "Yea, hath God said...?" in challenging what the Scriptures clearly teach as has so-called Christian psychology. From psychobabble-ized and Christianized 12-Steps programs (e.g., "Celebrate Recovery," which Saddleback has spread into thousands of churches) to the occult-ridden inner-healing ministries (e.g., Elijah House of John and Paula Sandford) to the humanistic self-teachings of Focus on the Family, the psycho-spiritual leaven spreads unabated.

The seeker-sensitive church-growth movement has pushed experientialism (and its close kin, pragmatism) into overdrive through the power of marketing. Sound doctrine, necessarily, is left by the wayside while churches meet the "felt needs" of consumers who are targeted as potential Christians.

Conviction of sin doesn't feel good, nor does it sell well. The wishful thinking of a purpose-driven church that would attract the lost by turning to the world's methods has become a *Titanic* that has ignored warnings and jettisoned its compass of the doctrine of Christ. While the orchestra searches for a contemporary chorus replacement for "Nearer My God To

Thee," the vessel is sinking into the depths of compromise while dispensing temporal lifejackets to save the world from its problems. This is the way that seems right to the world and to an astounding number of those who profess to believe the Bible.

Ironically, our day is seeing *more* Christian media and entertainment, and *more* Bibles of every sort—yet the result is a corruption of God's truth because there is no heart for sound biblical doctrine, especially since marketing departments are now leading the way! At best, the evangelical church in the U.S. reflects the lukewarmness of the Laodiceans (Revelation 3:14-17): rich and increased with experiential goods that can only yield shallow Christians; at worst, it has become a willing contributor to the end-times delusion.

Yet even in the face of so troubling a situation, we have reason to be both encouraged and fruitful; reason, that is, *if* we will obey Paul's inspired exhortation: "Take heed unto thyself, and unto the doctrine; continue in them: for in doing this thou shalt both save thyself, and them that hear thee [from the growing apostasy]" (1 Timothy 4:16). Let us pray for one another to that end.

---

*February 2007 (Originally titled
"Weaning Evangelicals Off the Word," part 1)*

2

CHANGING THE TRUTH INTO A LIE

If we say that we have fellowship with him, and walk in darkness, we lie, and do not the truth. . . . I have not written unto you because ye know not the truth, but because ye know it, and that <u>no lie is of the truth.</u>

— 1 JOHN 1:6, 2:21 —

In chapter 1, we quoted the Apostle Paul speaking about how Christians would view doctrine in the time prior to the return of Christ for His church: "For the time will come when they will not endure sound doctrine; but after their own lusts shall they heap to themselves teachers, having itching ears; and they shall turn away their ears from the truth, and shall be turned unto fables" (2 Timothy 4:3,4). Obviously, biblical doctrine will not be looked upon favorably. The implication is that doctrine will be regarded as rather burdensome, something that Christians of the future won't want to "endure." Conforming to sound doctrine involves spiritual discipline, thoughtful diligence, and making choices based on God's Word that go against the desires of the flesh.

What is sound doctrine? Very simply, it is the teachings of God, including His instructions, His precepts, His commandments—in short, it is every word that He says from Genesis to Revelation. "Man shall not live by bread alone, but by every word of God" (Luke 4:4). Yet in the Last Days, many if not most Christians will not endure sound doctrine.

So what will be left? Apostasy—a form of Christianity that is a mere shell of what the Bible teaches. It will accommodate the lusts of the flesh under the guise of godliness, as Paul tells us in his second epistle to Timothy. Furthermore, there will be an ample supply of persuasive Christians around who (whether intentionally or not) will subvert sound doctrine. And the process is already well underway.

As we pointed out in chapter 1, Satan's chief strategy in the seduction of mankind is to undermine, pervert, distort, corrupt, libel, denigrate, and deny the Scriptures by every possible means. The end product of his mission will be an apostate religion and church in which its adherents will worship and follow the Antichrist, the man of lawlessness whom Satan will empower. Fulfilling his mission involves a rather simple formula that was terribly effective in the Garden of Eden and throughout the Old Testament and apostolic times. It has continued throughout church history right up to our present day: to induce humanity to deviate from and then ultimately reject what God has said. Adam and Eve were the first to succumb. An inherited sin nature made their offspring easier prey for the adversary, the devil, who goes about as a roaring lion, "seeking whom he may devour" (1 Peter 5:8).

God continually declared to the Israelites that if they

obeyed Him they would be blessed, and if they walked in disobedience they would suffer the devastating consequences of
their sin: their own separation from God and God's separation
from them, the loss of righteous guidance and protection, and
the various disciplinary actions of God, including being sub-
jected to His wrath. Israel's wilderness experiences in Exodus
and through the cycles of rebellion and repentance in the
book of Judges testify to the fact that God is true to His word
and to His warnings. Deuteronomy seems to be an exercise
in redundancy as Moses again and again issues God's instructions to the children of Israel and cautions them to *carefully*
obey what He has commanded. It wasn't just a matter of law
but of *life*: "And he said unto them, Set your hearts unto all
the words which I testify among you this day, which ye shall
command your children to observe to do, all the words of this
law. For it is not a vain thing for you; because it is your life"
(Deuteronomy 32:46,47).

Samuel, the prophet and judge, echoes Moses' exhortation more than three centuries later: "Serve the Lord with
all your heart; and turn ye not aside: for then should ye go
after vain things, which cannot profit nor deliver; for they are
vain" (1 Samuel 12:20,21). Not only is turning from God a pursuit after vanity, something worthless, but the process itself is
wickedness: "For rebellion is as the sin of witchcraft, and stub-
bornness is as iniquity and idolatry" (1 Samuel 15:23). Samuel's
inspired analogy underscores not only the evil of rebellion as it
relates to idolatry, but it provides insight that helps us recognize Satan's *inducements* to disobedience, which are prevalent
in the church today.

Idolatry was the dominant issue. The children of Israel were commanded not to make graven images or gods of silver or gold (Exodus 20:3,4,23). What was their reply? "All that the LORD hath said will we do, and be obedient" (Exodus 24:7). Yet days later, when Moses failed to return from Mount Sinai and fear set in, they turned from the words of God to what they supposed would better meet their emotional and spiritual "felt needs." They fashioned a physical object to worship—a golden calf.

Although their act was unmitigated rebellion against God, let's consider what very likely influenced their thinking. Their spiritual leader had disappeared. Panic gripped them. They were more comfortable with the physical forms of worship learned from the Egyptians than with instructions from an invisible God. Perhaps Aaron thought that the best way to pacify the people was to give them something their physical senses could relate to—something *experientially* reassuring.

What's wrong with taking a wholistic approach, i.e., meeting the needs of body, mind, and spirit? Wouldn't their worship of a *physical* thing, as well as the *spiritual* stimulation of ritual, be "acceptable," as long as it was directed toward the God of Abraham, Isaac, and Jacob? Aaron must have thought so. He crafted a golden calf, built an altar, oversaw the liturgy, and dedicated the feast "unto the Lord." The Israelites' response was a precursor to the spirit of religious ecumenism and compromise so prevalent in our day, which is also based upon lies: "These be thy gods, O Israel, which brought thee up out of the land of Egypt" (Exodus 32:4).

We urgently need a biblical understanding of what idolatry comprises. Old Testament examples and the admonitions against it are given by God. Why would they be relevant for us? Because the evangelical church today is following Aaron's example! Most Christians would define idolatry as "whatever takes the place of God in our lives." True. Yet, too often, that rather general answer fails to help us understand the ways and means by which idolatry works. Consequently, we may not have the discernment necessary to be on our guard against it.

Why is understanding idolatry so important? Let's start with the obvious: The Bible defines idols as false gods (Psalm 96:5). They are items of deception and, even worse, the creations of men and devils. To worship them is delusion. The veneration itself often consists of debauchery and depravity, ritual activities completely given over to the physical senses. Idolatry involves materialism and experientialism, totally oriented toward the flesh. The so-called gods are physically represented and sensually worshiped. Most evangelicals know all this, but what many seem not to understand today is the *nature* of idolatry and how it subverts our worship of the true and living God.

The worship that God desired from the Israelites—His people, whom He set apart to receive His Messiah—stands in stark contrast to the religious endeavors of the heathen nations. Rather than giving them images, Moses spoke the *words* of God to them, and then he wrote the words in a Book. "And Moses wrote all the words of the Lord...and he took the book of the covenant, and read in the audience of the people" (Exodus 24:4,7). He told them (then wrote it down) that the making of images to represent God is condemned: "Thou shalt not make unto thee any graven image, or any likeness of any thing that is in heaven above, or that is in the earth beneath, or that is in the water under the earth: Thou shalt not bow down thyself to them, nor serve them" (Exodus 20:4-5).

Why would God give such a command? Because no image that man could ever draw, engrave, paint, sculpt, fashion through any medium, or conjure up in his mind, could truly represent Jehovah God. He is *infinite* (1 Kings 8:27). He is *spirit* (John 4:24). He is *invisible* (John 1:18). Even the God-prescribed places of worship were drastically different from their pagan counterparts. There was nothing physical to worship! The Holy of Holies within the tabernacle, and later in Solomon's temple, contained not the *image* of God but the *Word* of God, represented by the Ark of the Covenant. Contained within the Ark was the Testimony of God, the second set of tablets written by God's own hand (Deuteronomy 10:1,2). Again, by the design of God, the emphasis is on *the Word*.

God has chosen to reveal Himself to humanity through words, not images. In like manner, worship must be through *His Word*, according to *His Word*.

No doubt He selected words because they are best suited to convey precisely what He wants mankind to know and to do. Words have definite meanings and can be interpreted objectively. Only words, spoken or written, can come close to accurately communicating attributes of our transcendent God and His divine nature. On the other hand, worship aroused by imagery is based upon the imagination rather than upon the teachings of Scripture. Religious images can at best only convey information in a symbolic and superficial way. Their interpretations are mostly subjective, experiential, and rely mainly upon the imagination of the observer. The message of the Bible, however, is not about aesthetic gratification but about our redemption; it's not about our *feelings* but His *truth*—something that images can never express but only oppose. Jesus prayed to His Father for His disciples, "Sanctify them through thy truth: *thy word is truth*" (John 17:17).

The theology of the Bible is instructional. It is given in words so that man can understand it. "Wisdom is the principal thing; therefore get wisdom: and with all thy getting get understanding" (Proverbs 4:7). The Bible encourages faith that is founded upon evidence, logic, and reason. No image-reliant belief system can make those claims, and when the people of the Book turn to religious imagery, they are abandoning reason and following idolatry. That happened to the Israelites throughout their history, including when they were instructed by God to make a bronze serpent as a *symbol* that ultimately pointed to Christ's death on the Cross, in payment for the sins of the world. They later turned it into an object of idolatry and as a consequence God told them to destroy it (2 Kings 18:4).

Throughout its history, Christendom has likewise succumbed to idolatry through imagery and liturgical ritual. Roman Catholic tradition credits St. Veronica as having captured the image of Christ upon her veil, which supposedly became the source for later icons, paintings, and engravings of Jesus. St. Veronica continues to be venerated today when Catholics observe the ritual of the Stations of the Cross. Eastern Orthodoxy developed icons of Christ, Mary, and the Saints as devices for mystically transcending the temporal through imagery that enables one to "spiritually see" indescribable divinity. In the ninth century, the Russian Orthodox Church incorporated icons as a central part of their worship, including a form of divination known as "praying through the icons." Again, this is religious rebellion, which the Scriptures tell us is as the sin of witchcraft.

The Emperor Constantine did much to introduce idolatrous imagery into Christianity in order to appease the multitudes of pagans he coerced into joining his newly favored religion of the realm. It was during the Middle Ages, however, that the Roman Catholic Church greatly increased its use of visual imagery. Religious statues, paintings, reliefs, the display of relics, as well as expanded liturgies with the use of luxurious vestments, incense, candles, and processions were increasingly emphasized to encourage the participation of the mostly illiterate population. Rather than educate the people, the Church of Rome fed them an experiential, visual theology that prolonged their ignorance of the Scriptures and bred superstition. By God's grace, Gutenburg's printing press in the fifteenth century and the Reformation in the sixteenth century were instrumental in helping to turn those who "protested" against the abuses of the Catholic Church back to the Bible.

Astonishingly, the evangelical church is progressively sliding into idolatry as it turns from the Word of God to visual imagery. A goal of the American Bible Society is to put the entire Bible on video to accommodate our visually oriented generation (which has little interest in reading). *The Jesus Film*, a dramatic representation of the Gospel of Luke, has been the staple of Campus Crusade's overseas evangelical efforts. The very Catholic movie *The Passion of the Christ* became a runaway box-office hit, largely due to the overwhelming support it received from evangelicals. Biblically conservative mission organizations such as Gospel for Asia have used Mel Gibson's Hollywood production as part of its outreach program. Millions of *The Passion of the Christ* DVDs were purchased by evangelical churches for their Sunday schools, Bible studies, and small group meetings.

Religious movies are on the rise (e.g., *The Nativity Story, One Night with the King*) as evangelicals "partner" with Hollywood and demonstrate that they are an eager and profitable market. One pastor, whose church bought out theaters for private showings of *The Passion* (which produced only "one conversion") repented. He came under the conviction that rather than partnering with, his church was, in fact, "pimping for" Hollywood. As true as that may be, and as praiseworthy as his repentance was, if he doesn't understand the serious nature (as explained above) of attempting to represent God's Word in dramatic visual form, he is vulnerable to repeating the same error with visual idolatry.

This is not a blanket condemnation of the film/video medium, but films cannot be used to present the Scriptures visually without becoming idolatrous. Not only are the images historically false (they are conjured up from the imagination of a screenwriter or director), but they must also conform to the mechanics of the medium (acting, cinematography, art direction, lighting, music, sound effects, etc.), which are designed to manipulate the senses and the emotions for dramatic purposes (see *Showtime for the Sheep?* by this author).

Biblical movies are just one trend among dozens that are contributing to weaning evangelicals off the Word of God and producing biblically illiterate Christians. This is especially true regarding our visually oriented youth.

We serve a merciful God who can rescue a soul out of the darkest of circumstances but who will not support by His grace man's religious ways and means in their attempts to serve Him. "For my thoughts are not your thoughts, neither are your ways my ways, saith the LORD" (Isaiah 55:8). To the degree that we deviate from *His* way, we are lapsing into idolatry. As Jesus explained, "God is a Spirit and they that worship him must worship him in spirit and in truth" (John 4:24).

March 2007 (Originally titled
"Weaning Evangelicals Off the Word," part 2)

3

A Way Which
Seemeth Right

*But there were false prophets also among the people,
even as there shall be false teachers among you, who
privily shall bring in damnable heresies, even denying
the Lord that bought them, and bring upon themselves
swift destruction. And many shall follow their
pernicious ways; by reason of whom the way of truth
shall be evil spoken of.*

— 2 PETER 2:1-2 —

In the previous two chapters, I made some observations that
should be of great concern to those who consider themselves
Bible-believing Christians. Paul warned that there would come
a time when "sound doctrine" (2 Timothy 4:3,4) would give way to
what "seemeth right unto a man" (Proverbs 14:12) in determining
what is true. There will be apostate "teachers" who advance
an experiential mode that panders to the lusts of the flesh,
promoting self-serving "fables" or myths. Furthermore, these

"deceitful workers" and lying "ministers of righteousness" (2 Corinthians 11:13,15) would draw upon the teachings of "seducing spirits, and doctrines of devils" (1 Timothy 4:1). Paul certainly had such teachers in mind as he warned the Ephesian elders that after his departing "grievous wolves" would enter among them and teach "perverse things, to draw away disciples after them" (Acts 20: 29,30). There is no doubt that these verses are being fulfilled in our day.

Although there are far too many examples of apostasy influencing the church today to cite in this brief series of articles, there is one spurious trend that encompasses nearly all of what the above verses address. It's called the Emerging Church Movement (ECM). The ECM is a development among evangelicals that appears to have some worthwhile goals: 1) It professes to speak to today's culture about the relevancy of Christianity and the value of the gospel of Jesus Christ; and 2) It desires to keep young evangelicals continuing in the faith. The movement involves a number of churches (mostly non-denominational), some supportive ministries and parachurch organizations, and the support of a number of prominent evangelical leaders and authors.

The ECM has no official organization or leadership, although some of its adherents have "emerged" as recognized leaders and spokesmen. For many of those helping to promote the movement, their motivation to "try something different" grew out of the frustration of their own very limited success in evangelizing and discipling young people. Some of the leaders were in seeker-sensitive and purpose-driven churches, and they saw firsthand that their church-growth marketing schemes were not effective for drawing those in their late teens, 20s, and early 30s. The main fare of most consumer-driven churches features contemporary music with shallow, repetitive choruses, topical 30-minutes-or-less sermons (mostly psychology-based), a host of social programs to attract the lost (and the fleshly nature of Christians), and "Bible studies" that address everything but the Bible. For a surprising number of young adults, that was a spiritual turnoff.

In his book *The Emerging Church* (with contributions and endorsement by Rick Warren), Dan Kimball relates his own breakthrough in overcoming the frustrating experiences in trying to motivate the young people in the evangelical church where he was youth pastor. He tells about watching a concert on the youth-oriented MTV network late one night that was a candlelit, all-acoustic performance. Recognizing that MTV certainly knows its audience and the youth culture, he refashioned his church's youth room into a subdued, "catacombish," candlelit environment and had the worship band use acoustic guitars, forgoing their usual flashing light show and loud electric music. He was delighted by the reaction of one usually unresponsive teen who said, "I like this. This was really spiritual."

That was an epiphany for Kimball. As he expanded the service with what he considered more "authentic Christian" elements and liturgy, it attracted hundreds, young and old alike. He is convinced he's found what the church of today needs: "As the emerging church returns to a rawer and more vintage form of Christianity, we may see explosive growth much like the early church did."

On the contrary, the "explosive growth" in the early church came from an approach that is almost nonexistent in the ECM. Peter's confrontational address to the crowd on Pentecost in Acts chapter 2 is directly at odds with the *modus operandi* of the emergent leaders. In the power of the Holy Spirit, Peter's preaching brought conviction of sin, repentance, and belief; 3,000 came to Christ that day. Kimball's "vintage form of Christianity," featuring rituals, ceremony, candles, incense, prayer stations, and images to create a spiritually experiential atmosphere for evangelicals is "vintage" only in the sense that it is an imitation of the later unbiblical Eastern Orthodox and medieval Roman Catholic liturgies. The early New Testament church knew nothing of this idolatrous and sense-oriented worship.

Ironically, emergent churches around the world, in their attempt to "reconstruct" the church, are passing each other like ships in the night. Kimball's efforts at spiritual stimulation by introducing to young evangelicals the liturgical bells and smells of Catholic, Orthodox, Lutheran, and high-church Episcopal and Presbyterian rituals, stands in contradiction to some European cathedrals and churches going emergent. Europeans are trying to revive their congregations, deadened by centuries of imagery and ritual, by covering their gothic interiors with decorated drapery, exchanging the organ and traditional hymns for electric guitars and contemporary choruses, and adding throw pillows for comfortable seating to create a seeker-friendly environment. These churches are abandoning the very things that are "spiritually" alluring to American emergent evangelicals. Regarding both sensual approaches, Scripture tells us, "the flesh profiteth nothing."

In reading the works of the ECM leaders, we would agree with many of their criticisms of current Christianity. There is plenty to oppose as apostasy and the abandonment of the Word increases in Christendom. The ECM's corrections, however, rather than having restorative value for the church, are just as contrary to the Scriptures. Even worse, they go far beyond subtly "weaning evangelicals off the Word" to rendering the Bible and its doctrines as *the enemy* when it comes to drawing the world in general and, specifically, our postmodern culture, to the love of Jesus.

The Emergent Church Movement claims to desire—above all things—to show the love and life of Christ to a culture that is distrustful of the Christianity it perceives as oppressive and absolutist. We're assured by ECM writers that "numbers of postmoderns are attracted to Jesus but detest His church" and can therefore be reached by the emerging church approach. It professes to be more amenable to the culture, more viable in its practice of Christianity, and truer to what Jesus had in mind for His church on earth.

Admirable—but let's see how true it is to the Scriptures. As Isaiah exhorted, "To the law and to the testimony [i.e., God's Word]: if they speak not according to this word, it is because there is no light in them" (Isaiah 8:20).

First of all, one has to wonder what a postmodern—a person characterized chiefly by his or her general disdain for authority and absolutes, particularly those dealing with moral issues and religion—thinks about this "Jesus" to whom he or she is supposedly drawn. The critical question is "Jesus who?" Is it the *biblical* Jesus they like—the one who declared absolutely, "I am the way, the truth, and the life: no man cometh unto the Father but by me" (John 14:6)? What about the *authoritarian* Jesus, who announced, "If ye keep my commandments, ye shall abide in my love" (John 15:10)? His words weren't referring only to the Ten Commandments but rather to every *instruction* He gave. Is that the Jesus a postmodern desires? What about the Jesus who gave mankind an ultimatum: "He that believeth on the Son hath everlasting life: and he that believeth not the Son shall not see life; but the wrath of God abideth on him" (John 3:36)?

The biblical Jesus certainly does not accommodate postmodernism, which is one more example of humanity's rebellion against its Creator. The good news is that Jesus offers deliverance from the delusion of postmodernism, as well as all the other man-centered *isms*: "If ye continue in my word, then are ye my disciples indeed; and ye shall know the truth, and the truth shall make you free" (John 8:31,32). The bad news is that the emerging church approach attempts to accommodate Jesus and the Scriptures (actually "another Jesus" and a corrupted and emasculated Word) to our postmodern culture.

Although some regard the Emerging Church Movement as nothing more than a passing spiritual fad among young evangelicals, its potential for shipwrecking the faith of our next generation (should the Lord not yet return for His saints) is staggering. Here are just a few of the faith-destroying beliefs as espoused in the writings of the emergent leaders. First of all, foundational to the ECM is the subversion of the Bible. It's akin to Satan's scheme to destabilize Eve's trust in what God commanded: "Yea, hath God said...?" (Genesis 3:1). They give lip service to the importance of God's Word while undermining its inerrancy, authority, and sufficiency.

Rob Bell writes in *Velvet Elvis*, following 22 pages of weakening the authority of the Bible (making statements such as "It is possible to make the Bible say whatever we want it to, isn't it?" and "With God being so massive and awe-inspiring and full of truth, why is his book capable of so much confusion?"): "[L]et's make a group decision to drop once and for all the Bible-as-owner's-manual metaphor [i.e., God's specific instructions for mankind]. It's terrible. It really is....We have to embrace the Bible as the wild, uncensored, passionate account it is of experiencing the living God."[1] No! "Holy men of God spake as they were moved by the Holy Ghost" (2 Peter 1:21).

His view, common to most emergent writers, is that the key to the authority of Scripture is one's interpretation, and that is most authoritative when the interpretation takes place in a community and validated by a "group decision": "Community, community, community. Together with others, wrestling and searching and engaging the Bible as a group of people hungry to know God in order to follow God."[2]

Although we find, thousands of times throughout the Bible, clear, direct, and absolute commands prefaced by phrases such as "Thus saith the Lord" and "The word of the Lord came to me," we're now told that understanding and obedience to what God said are subject to a community's interpretation. Consequently, ECM churches disdain preaching and authoritative teaching, yet they delight in discussion, causing some to dump the pulpit in favor of a dialogue-led Starbucks environment. As the goals of the community change, we're told the interpretation may also change.

The claim that the ECM approach has not jettisoned sound doctrine is either a delusion or an outright deception. This becomes clear when one asks for a biblical position on an issue. Kristen Bell acknowledges in a *Christianity Today* emerging church article, "I grew up thinking that we figured out the Bible...that we knew what it means. Now I have no idea what most of it means, and yet I feel like life is big again—like life used to be black and white, and now it's in color."[3] Brian McLaren, the most prominent of the emergent leaders, echoes Bell's "doctrine" of avoidance regarding what the Bible says about homosexuality:

> Perhaps we need a five-year moratorium on making [doctrinal] pronouncements. In the meantime, we'll practice prayerful Christian dialogue, listening respectfully, disagreeing agreeably. When decisions need to be made, they'll be admittedly provisional. We'll keep our ears attuned to scholars in biblical studies, theology, ethics, psychology, genetics, sociology, and related fields. Then in five years, if we have clarity, we'll speak; if not, we'll set another five years for ongoing reflection.[4]

TBC has received numerous letters from parents and evangelical pastors who find their young people seeking out emergent churches for the "new" experiences, which they offer in abundance: religious art (primarily impressionistic images of "Jesus"), "biblical" films, rituals based upon Catholic/Orthodox liturgy, community, personal relationships, contemplative spirituality and mysticism (some include yoga), Bible dialogues, ecumenical interaction with "people of faith," a social gospel, plans to save the planet, restore the kingdom, and so forth.

Regarding the seductive nature of such things, few evangelicals, young or old, have a defense. Too many function as biblical illiterates, meaning they know some things about the Bible and are capable of reading it but simply haven't made any effort, outside of following along with their pastor's teaching on Sundays. They are the spiritual con man's delight.

Satan's seduction of Eve began subtly, "Yea hath God said?" It was a confusion tactic, setting her up to believe his lie and reject what God had said: "And the serpent said unto the woman, Ye shall not surely die." That was his punch line to destroy the human race. Eve fell for it; Adam went along.

One finds a strikingly similar approach in the writings of the ECM leaders in regard to destroying faith in the gospel: Brian McLaren leads with doubts about what God had said:

> The church latched on to that old doctrine of original sin like a dog to a stick, and before you knew it, the whole gospel got twisted around it. Instead of being God's big message of saving love for the whole world, the gospel became a little bit of secret information on how to solve the pesky legal problem of original sin.[5]

He says elsewhere, "I don't think we've got the gospel right yet. What docs it mcan to be saved?...None of us have arrived at orthodoxy."

British emergent leader and Zondervan author Steve Chalke delivers the punch line that unabashedly rejects the essential gospel belief that Christ paid the full penalty for the sins of mankind necessary to satisfy divine justice. Incredibly, he condemns that doctrine as a form of "cosmic child abuse" and a "twisted version of events morally dubious and a huge barrier to faith."[6] This is where these emergent pied pipers, wittingly or unwittingly, are seductively leading our youth.

Hopefully, the above will move you to prayer and action regarding the biblical strengthening of your own children and the youth in your fellowship.

September 2007 (Originally titled,
"Weaning Evangelicals Off the Word" part 3)

4

EVANGELICAL MYSTICISM?

The light of the body is the eye: if therefore thine eye
be single, thy whole body shall be full of light.
But if thine eye be evil, thy whole body shall be full
of darkness. If therefore the light that is in thee be
darkness, how great is that darkness!

—MATTHEW 6:22-23—

I find myself increasingly grieved these days by what I see taking place among those who profess to be evangelicals. I know the term "evangelical" has undergone radical changes regarding its meaning and practice. Yet when I use the term, I'm going by a very simple definition: I'm referring to those who claim to accept the Bible alone as their authority for knowing and receiving God's way of salvation and for living their lives in a way that is pleasing to Him.

Thirty years ago, it was young adult evangelicals who were used wonderfully by the Lord to help open my eyes to the fact that I was eternally separated from God and that the religious system I was depending on to get me to heaven was a false hope. That wasn't easy for me to accept at the time. Although my commitment to the Roman Catholic Church had weakened during my late twenties, the attitude, "I was born a Catholic, I'll die a Catholic," was woven into the fabric of my mind.

As I think back on those days, I recognize that I was a young man in bondage. Certainly, I was in bondage to sin, as is everyone who is not born again. But there was another bondage that also gripped me: the bondage of Roman Catholic tradition, with its sacraments, liturgies, rituals, and sacramentals. Not only were such things unbiblical—they were works of the flesh and devices of demons. In my own life, as well as throughout the history of the Church of Rome, they were soul-gripping superstitions advanced under the guise of spirituality.

I trusted in relics of dead so-called Saints; holy water; making the sign of the cross; votive candles; baptism for salvation (infant or otherwise); a "transubstantiated" piece of bread alleged to be Christ; apparitions of Mary; a scapular; a "miraculous medal"; statues and images of Jesus, Mary, and the saints; endless Rosaries, Novenas, the Stations of the Cross; abstaining from meat on Friday; Lenten abstinences; the Last Rites to get me into Purgatory and indulgences to get me out of Purgatory; Mass cards; graces dispensed from Mary; the confessional, with absolution of my sins by a priest; penance and personal suffering to purify me of my sin; worshiping a piece of bread at the Eucharistic Holy Hour; the Holy Father as the Vicar of Christ on earth, etc., etc. Therein lies a bondage that few evangelicals understand.

Many brush these things aside as non-essentials of the

Christian faith or minor theological aberrations unique to Catholicism. Not true. They are essential to the gospel that Rome declares—a gospel of meritorious works that the Bible condemns (see Galatians, Romans, Ephesians, et al.) as a rejection of the completed substitutionary atonement of Christ our Savior. Catholicism's Tradition, which is declared to be equal in authority to Scripture, is made up of those things (such as cited above) that are necessary for, or supportive of, a Catholic's entrance into heaven.

According to the Word of God, anything that is added to Christ's finished work on the cross is a denial of the gospel: that Christ paid the *full penalty* for the sins of humanity.

The Roman Catholic Church, which claims infallibility in its Councils and theological teachings, clearly and emphatically denies the biblical gospel. The Council of Trent declares:

> 6th Session, Canon 9: If anyone says that the sinner is justified by faith alone, meaning that nothing else is required to cooperate in order to obtain the grace of justification...let him be anathema.

> 6th Session, Canon 12: If anyone shall say that justifying faith is nothing else than confidence in the divine mercy which remits sins for Christ's sake, or that it is this confidence alone by which we are justified: let him be anathema.

> 6th Session, Canon 30: If anyone says that after the reception of the grace of justification the guilt is so remitted and the debt of eternal punishment so blotted out to every repentant sinner, that no debt of temporal punishment remains to be

discharged either in this world or in purgatory before the gates of heaven can be opened, let him be anathema.

7th Session, Canon 4: If anyone says that the sacraments of the New Law [canons and decrees of the Church] are not necessary for salvation but... without them...men obtain from God through faith alone the grace of justification...let him be anathema.

"Anathema," in these decrees (which are still in force), damns to hell anyone who rejects the Roman Catholic Church's false gospel of works.

Starting with the Second Vatican Council in the 1960s, where only superficial changes were made (because infallible dogmas cannot be changed!), Rome launched an ecumenical program aimed at seducing Protestants worldwide and, specifically, evangelicals in the United States. The goal was and is to bring all of Christendom under the rule of the Roman Catholic Church with the pope as its spiritual head. Predictable progress has been made in Europe and the U.S. among liberal denominations that have long abandoned the Scriptures. Astonishing, however, is the success the scheme has had among American evangelicals.

Billy Graham was the first and most notable evangelical to support Catholicism's ecumenical efforts. Others followed, including Bill Bright, Pat Robertson, J. I. Packer, Timothy George, Robert Schuller, Hank Hanegraaff, Benny Hinn, and Jack Van Impe. Evangelicals and Catholics Together, under the leadership of Chuck Colson and Catholic priest Richard John Neuhaus, declared Catholics and evangelicals to be "brothers and sisters in Christ" and exhorted them to work together in spreading the gospel. Obviously, and conveniently, that gospel was never defined.

Although the acceptance of things Roman Catholic among evangelicals grew steadily over the years after Vatican II, it increased exponentially with the popularity of ultra-conservative Catholic Mel Gibson's *The Passion of the Christ*. His dramatization of one of Catholicism's most sacred rituals, The Stations of the Cross, so captured the hearts of evangelicals that their eagerness to purchase mass quantities of tickets accounted for the movie's great financial success. Following that achievement, *Inside the Vatican* made this insightful observation: "For evangelicals, the film has given them a glimpse inside the Catholic soul, even the traditional Catholic soul. Many evangelicals, reflecting on what they saw in the movie, say they are beginning to 'get' the whole Catholic thing: Lent...the ashes on the forehead...no meat on Friday...the sorrowful mysteries...the Stations of the Cross...the emphasis on the Eucharist...the devotion to Mary...the enormous crucifix hanging above every Catholic altar. They may not be rushing out to buy rosaries, necessarily, but some of the things no longer seem so strange, so alien."[1]

What evangelicals also "got," which their leaders enthusiastically endorsed as "biblically accurate," were numerous scenes based upon the imagination of an 18th-century Catholic mystic, the portrayal of Mary as co-redemptrix in the salvation of mankind, and a very Catholic gospel that has Christ atoning for sin by suffering the unrelenting physical tortures of the Roman soldiers.[2]

The Passion of the Christ had a stunning effect on evangelical youth and youth pastors. Not only did "[Catholic] things no longer seem so strange, so alien," but they were showing up in the youth ministries of evangelical churches. The Stations of the Cross ritual became popular, although it needed to be downsized from 14 stations to 11, eliminating some stations that were too foreign to Scripture (such as Saint Veronica capturing the image of Christ's bloodied face on her veil). Prayer altars were erected, featuring icons illuminated by candles and fragranced by burning incense, and prayer labyrinths were painted on large tarps placed in church basements or cut into church lawns. For young evangelicals too often raised on empty, repetitive worship choruses little different from secular music, and religious instruction leaning heavily upon entertainment to keep them interested, the Catholic and Orthodox liturgies seemed far more spiritual.

This all became "spiritual" fodder for the Emerging Church Movement (ECM), much of it a reaction against the consumer-oriented marketing approach to church growth popularized by Robert Schuller, Bill Hybels, and Rick Warren. Many ECM leaders, most of whom have evangelical backgrounds, saw Catholic ritual and mysticism as a necessary spiritual ingredient that was lost for evangelicals at the Reformation. *Sola Scriptura* was a major rallying cry of the Reformers against the abuses stemming from Roman Catholic tradition; the Bible as one's only authority practically shut down the influence of the Catholic mystics known as the Desert Fathers.

Yet Catholic mysticism has returned with a vengeance. Its occult techniques can be found nearly everywhere, from Youth Specialities to Richard Foster's Renovaré organization to Rick Warren's *Purpose Driven Life*. "Many Christian leaders started searching for a new approach under the banner of 'spiritual formation.' This new search has led many of them back to Catholic contemplative practices and medieval monastic disciplines," Brian McLaren writes approvingly.

Tony Jones, co-editor of *An Emergent Manifesto of Hope* has written a manifesto of mysticism for emerging churches titled *The Sacred Way: Spiritual Practices for Everyday Life*. Jones's acknowledgement of those who supported his effort reads as a *Who's Who* of emergent leaders, not to mention the Catholic priests he thanks and the ancient Orthodox and Catholic mystics he quotes. What then is this mysticism they are promoting?

Catholic mysticism is thoroughly subjective and experiential. Like its parent, Eastern mysticism, it claims that God can neither be known nor understood through human reason but only *experienced* subjectively through various techniques. It is the antithesis of what the Bible teaches: "Come now, and let us reason together, saith the LORD" (Isaiah 1:18); "Wisdom is the principal thing; therefore get wisdom: and with all thy getting get understanding" (Proverbs 4:7); "According as his divine power hath given unto us all things that pertain unto life and godliness, through the knowledge of him" (2 Peter 1:3). Furthermore, the goal of mysticism is union with God, i.e., the merging of one's soul into God. This is an impossibility that reveals mysticism's pantheistic and *panentheistic* roots, that God is everything and is in everything. No. God is infinite and transcendent, absolutely separate from His finite creation.

The Sacred Way endorses numerous mystical techniques that are gaining acceptance among evangelicals today. An awareness and understanding of them is therefore critical for discernment. *Centering Prayer* utilizes a single word (e.g., "love" or "God") upon which one focuses to clear the mind of all other thoughts. The belief is that the so-called pray-er will hear directly from God in his silence before Him. Tony Campolo declares, "In my case intimacy with Christ has developed gradually over the years, primarily through what Catholic mystics call 'centering prayer.' Each morning, as soon as I wake up, I take time—sometimes as much as a half hour—to center myself on Jesus. I say his name over and over again to drive back the 101 things that begin to clutter up my mind the minute I open my eyes. Jesus is my mantra, as some would say."[3]

The *Jesus Prayer* has the pray-er repeat a sentence such as "Lord Jesus, have mercy on me" continuously, hundreds—even thousands—of times. The repetition supposedly fixates one's mind upon Jesus. Yet it blatantly rejects His command not to use vain repetition in prayer as the heathen do (Matthew 6:7). Moreover, its constant repetitions turn prayer as a form of communication with Jesus into an act of nonsense.

Lectio Divina, meaning "sacred reading," is a technique that is far removed from normal reading and studying of the Bible. Its methodology aims at going beyond the objective meaning of the words and the straightforward instructions to that which transcends normal awareness. Jones writes, "As you attend to those deeper meanings, begin to meditate on the feelings and emotions conjured up in your inner self."[4] He then summarizes this mystical contemplative technique: "True contemplation moves beyond words and intellect and into that 'thin space' where time and eternity almost touch. It's in moments like these that some of the greatest [Catholic] saints in the history of the [Catholic] church have had a 'mystical union' with Christ."[5] It's clear from God's Word that the spirit with which they had a "mystical union" in their contemplative altered state of consciousness was not Jesus.

Ignatian Examen is an occult visualization technique taught by Ignatius Loyola, who founded the Jesuits in the 16th century. His exercise teaches one to visualize oneself in the presence of Jesus and then interact with Him during his earthly events, e.g., "at the Last Supper and the Garden of Gethsemane, at the foot of the cross, and laying Jesus' body in the tomb."[6] This has one adding content to Scripture from his imagination and opens a person to demonic manipulation (2 Corinthians 11:4; Galatians 1:8).

Prayer Labyrinths are concentric paths created by the Catholic Church in the 13th century to experience in one's imagination Christ's *Via Dolorosa*, or "walk of sorrows," when He carried His cross to Calvary's hill. Rather than subject themselves to the dangers of a pilgrimage to Jerusalem during Holy Week, Roman Catholics in Europe could gain the same indulgences (to shorten their time in Purgatory) by walking labyrinths at certain cathedrals while prayerfully meditating upon Christ's crucifixion. Likewise, observing the "sacred" ritual of the Stations of the Cross became a substitute for a pilgrimage to the Holy Land.

As a former Catholic, it's hard for me to fathom the evangelical church buying into the religious occultism of Roman Catholicism. It makes no sense. Visit any country where that religion is taken seriously. What becomes obvious is a people who are in the bondage of superstition. On the other hand, I shouldn't be surprised. Apostasy is growing rapidly, the religion of the Antichrist is taking shape, and mysticism, whether it's the Catholic variety, the Sufism of Islam, yoga and the gurus of Eastern mysticism, the Shamanism of native religions, or otherwise, is a common yet powerful magnet that draws all religions together.

We need to be watchmen on the wall as we see this evil invading the church, warning especially—should our Lord delay His return—our next generation of believers. They are the clear targets of this mystical seduction.

_____

February 2008

5

ANCIENT-FUTURE HERESIES

*I marvel that ye are so soon removed from him that
called you into the grace of Christ unto another gospel:
Which is not another; but there be some that trouble
you, and would pervert the gospel of Christ.*

— GALATIANS 1:6-7 —

Here's an idea. Let's go back through historical church eras
and glean from such time periods those issues deemed
to be of value in the development of the Christian faith. Let's
review the first-century church, the church between A.D. 100
and 600, then consider the medieval era (A.D. 700 to 1500),
followed by the Reformation period (A.D. 1500 and later),
and so on. To be effective in this endeavor, it's important to
have a good understanding of the cultural context in which the
Christians of each era practiced their faith. In addition, we'll
need to study the Church Fathers and gain the insights they
provided. Why? Well, those who are promoting this "re-pre-
senting the past" believe that today's Christianity will greatly
benefit as it "re-invents itself" in order to effectively bring the

message of the gospel to the postmodern world. If you think this may not be a good idea, you could be labeled a "traditionalist," one whose faith and practice is inflexible and out of touch with our rapidly changing culture—and church.

That's the view that *Christianity Today* (*CT*) has of what's going on in evangelical Christianity. In introducing its February 2008 feature article with a cover-page declaration, "Lost Secrets of the Ancient Church: How evangelicals started looking backward to move forward," *CT* senior managing editor Mark Galli writes:

> You might say a number of *CT* editors have a vested interest in this issue's cover story. David Neff, Ted Olsen, Tim Morgan, and I have been doing the ancient-future thing for many years, at Episcopal and/or Anglican parishes. And if this were not enough immersion in the topic, in his spare time, David Neff heads up the Robert E. Webber Center for an Ancient Evangelical Future, founded by the father of the ancient-future movement.

Acknowledging the magazine's inherent (and *historic*) bias, Galli notes that "the ancient church has captivated the evangelical imagination for some time [yet] it hasn't been until recently that it's become an *accepted fixture* of the evangelical landscape. And this is *for the good*" (emphasis added). That, of course, is Galli's opinion and, sadly, a growing multitude of influential Christian leaders agree.

Robert E. Webber, who died [in 2007], is certainly the

"father of the ancient-future movement," and his many books have provided encouragement and content for leaders of Emerging Church fellowships. As a Wheaton College professor for three decades, he also played a significant part in influencing that evangelical institution's capitulation to ecumenism, particularly its support of Roman Catholicism.

Webber wrote in his book, *Ancient-Future Faith: Rethinking Evangelicalism for a Postmodern World*, "Currently, Western society is in a transition from the modern world to a postmodern world...shifting us toward the affirmation of new values... resulting in a whole new culture and rais[ing] new questions about the way a biblical Christianity is to be understood and communicated."[1] The solution for Christianity to be viable in this cultural transition, Webber contends, is to "recover the universally accepted framework of faith that originated with the apostles, was developed by the [Church] Fathers, and has been handed down by the church in its liturgical and theological traditions."[2]

This Church Fathers' "framework of faith," along with "its liturgical and theological traditions" is found primarily, according to Webber, in the era of "Classic Christianity," between A.D. 100 and 600. And it was to that church age that most of the speakers at the 2007 Wheaton Theology Conference on "The Ancient Faith for the Church's Future" sang their praises. CT describes what took place at the Billy Graham Center in the Cliff Barrows Auditorium, including taking the audience through prayers from the *Gelasian Sacramentary* (also known as the *Book of Sacraments of the Church of Rome*), a fifth-century book of Catholic liturgy containing the priest's instructions for celebrating the Eucharist and recommending them for worship in today's Protestant churches. One speaker promoted the Catholic "medieval fourfold hermeneutic," which emphasizes the nonliteral interpretation of the Bible, and another "gleefully passed on the news" to this highly receptive crowd "that Liberty University had observed the liturgical season of Lent."

The writer of the article then asks, "Had Catholics taken over?" in this former bastion of conservative evangelicalism. His answer is NO! This Wheaton College conference was simply evangelicals looking to the past for "rich biblical, spiritual, and theological treasures to be found within the early church" as supplied by the early Church Fathers.[3]

Are evangelicals truly paying attention to the Church Fathers? University professor D. H. Williams, author of *Evangelicals and Tradition*, substantiated "the recent upsurge of evangelical interest in patristics (the study of the Church Fathers): 'Who would have thought, a decade ago, that one of the most vibrant and serious fields of Christian study at the beginning of the 21st century would be the ancient church fathers? There has been an opening of new avenues...[created] by the almost overnight popularity of bishops and monks, martyrs and apologists, philosophers and historians who first fashioned a Christian culture 1,500 years ago.'"[4]

Although these developments may seem shockingly new to some and seem to have sprung up overnight, *Christianity Today* gives some preparatory background. The article quotes Robert Webber from his then controversial 1978 book *Common Roots*: "My argument is that the era of the early church (A.D. 100-500), and particularly the second century, contains insights which evangelicals need to recover." *CT* notes that 25 years later Webber rejoiced in his book Younger Evangelicals that they [emergent fellowships] "want to immerse themselves in the past and form a culture that is connected to the past...."

Nearly a decade earlier than *Common Roots*, a number of Campus Crusade leaders went on their own "recovery" of ancient liturgies, specifically from Eastern Orthodoxy. Peter Gillquist, Jack Sparks, Jon Braun, and others left Campus Crusade to form what was a forerunner of today's ancient-future-emergent movement. They turned to the writings of the early Church Fathers "to practice a more liturgical form of worship than in their previous evangelical background."[5] They called their movement the New Covenant Apostolic Order and, later, the Evangelical Orthodox Church.

In 1978, Quaker and *CT* advisory editor Richard Foster wrote *Celebration of Discipline*. His book, which introduced Catholic and occult meditative techniques to evangelicals, sold more than a million copies and was selected by *Christianity Today* as one of the top ten books of the 20th century. Foster later formed Renovaré, an organization dedicated to teaching spiritual formation through the mystical beliefs and practices of the Eastern Orthodox and Roman Catholic Desert Fathers. Eugene Peterson (*CT* editor), author of the very popular paraphrased Bible, *The Message,* was the New Testament editor of the *Renovaré Spiritual Formation Bible*.

These developments are foundational to today's Emerging Church phenomenon and indicate that such roots will carry it well beyond its merely being a fad among today's evangelical youth. More recent support, as previously mentioned, is the change in attitude among evangelicals toward Roman Catholicism fostered by "Evangelicals & Catholics Together: The Christian Mission in the Third Millennium," an endeavor of Chuck Colson and Father Richard John Neuhaus (both *CT* editors) and the stunning success (thanks to evangelicals) of Mel Gibson's extremely Catholic *The Passion of the Christ.*

Is any of this "for the good," as *Christianity Today* declares?

Let's both reason from the Scriptures, and simply be reasonable (Isaiah 1:18). The Ancient-Future search to discover gems from "Classic Christianity" comes up short by a century—the century in which the New Testament was written. The critical difference should be obvious. The writers of the New Testament were *inspired by the Holy Spirit* as they penned God's Word (2 Timothy 3:16; 2 Peter 1:21,22). What writings from A.D. 100 and later can claim such inspiration? None. But we're told that some were disciples of or lived at the time of the apostles. True, but proximity to the apostles is hardly a guarantee against heresy nor does it come close to inspiration. Furthermore, much of the first-century-written New Testament reproved and corrected errors that had *already entered the church!*

Remember the Apostle Paul's warning to the Ephesian elders, who were certainly closer to Paul than any of the so-called Church Fathers:

> Take heed therefore unto yourselves, and to all the flock, over the which the Holy Ghost hath made you overseers, to feed the church of God, which he hath purchased with his own blood. For I know this, that after my departing shall grievous wolves enter in among you, not sparing the flock. Also

> of your own selves shall men arise, speaking per-
> verse things, to draw away disciples after them.
> Therefore watch, and remember, that by the space
> of three years I ceased not to warn every one night
> and day with tears. (Acts 20:28-31)

Again, why this attraction to the ancient Church Fathers? Could any of them say with Paul, "Those things, which ye have both learned, and received, and heard, and seen in me, do: and the God of peace shall be with you" (Philippians 4:9)? We can trust his God-breathed words *completely*. On the other hand, it takes very little scrutiny of men like Origen, Irenaeus, Tertullian, Clement of Alexandria, Cyprian, Justin Martyr, Athanasius, John Chrysostom, Cyril of Jerusalem, Augustine, and others, to see their flaws, let alone their heresies. For example, Origen taught that God would save everyone and that Mary was a perpetual virgin; Irenaeus believed that the bread and wine became the body and blood of Jesus when consecrated, as did John Chrysostom and Cyril of Jerusalem; Athanasius taught salvation through baptism; Tertullian became a sup-porter of the Montanist heresies, and a promoter of a New Testament clergy class, as did his disciple Cyprian; Augustine was the principal architect of Catholic dogma that included his support of purgatory, baptismal regeneration, and infant baptism, mortal and venial sins, prayers to the dead, penance for sins, absolution from a priest, the sinlessness of Mary, the Apocrypha as Scripture, etc.

It's not that these men got everything wrong; some, on certain doctrines, upheld Scripture against the developing unbiblical dogmas of the Roman Catholic Church. Nevertheless, overall they are a heretical minefield. So why seek them out?

Worse yet are the Desert Fathers and the Catholic mystics. Anthony the Great, known as the father of Christian monasticism, is the most revered of the Desert Fathers. According to Athanasius, the devil fought Anthony by afflicting him with boredom, laziness, and the phantoms of women, which he countered by becoming a hermit and isolating himself for years inside a tomb. He communicated with the outside world through a crevice that enabled him to receive food and to offer spiritual advice. Supposedly, the devil, upset by his holiness, would come and beat him unmercifully.

Later mystics were no less bizarre—or unbiblical. Benedictine nun Julian of Norwich, a favorite of evangelical mystic wannabes and "Christian" feminists, believed in universal salvation, that God was in all things, referred to God as "Father-Mother," and experienced intense visions of heaven and hell. Her most famous saying became a positive mental attitude mantra: "All shall be well, and all shall be well, and all manner of thing shall be well." Like Anthony, she had herself walled off from society, living for 20 years in a cell attached to a church, where a small window provided access to food and a view of the church altar and of the Eucharist.

Could these hermits and mystics really interest evangelicals? *Christianity Today* says they do. Referring to "monastic evangelicals" and the "new monasticism," an insert in its cover article observes how "growing numbers of evangelicals" are "taking their newfound love affair with Christian tradition" beyond "books and talk" and are "now experimenting with advent candles [and] sampling [Catholic] practices associated with Lent...." *CT* credits Richard Foster's *Devotional Classics* as possibly fueling this latest trend, and it notes that Brian McLaren, Tony Jones, and a number of emerging church writers have "been calling evangelicals to monastic models as a guide for the future."[6]

As a former Roman Catholic, I am staggered when I see who and what *Christianity Today* is blatantly promoting. Robert Webber, for example, writes in *Signs and Wonders* of an experience that changed his Protestant life. He received the Eucharist (allegedly the "actual body and blood of Christ under the appearance of bread and wine") while at a Catholic retreat center: "You might say I was surprised by joy!...I had never had an experience like that in my life....I had been in dialog with another worship tradition, and I was surely the richer for it"[7] Thousands of steadfast biblical Christians were martyred for refusing that idolatrous and gospel-denying "worship tradition."

Campus Crusade leader-turned-Orthodox-priest Peter Gillquist explains the "mission" he and those who joined him are on: "Our desire is to make North America Orthodox!" As former conservative evangelicals, they believe that "if we [could] become Orthodox, then anyone in North America can!" Furthermore, due to their apologetics and evangelism training, "...we represent a strong force for *Orthodox* evangelization....And we know there are many others just like us who if given the time and persuasion will join the Orthodox ranks just as we have."[8]

Will this soon pass? No. It's all part of related agendas that are building the end-times apostate church (Revelation 13:8). Its tools are experientialism, subjectivism, mysticism, and dominionism, all of which aggressively and obstinately subvert the Word of God. They are intentionally (in some cases unwittingly) being used to work out Satan's primary scheme against God and mankind (Genesis 3:1: "Yea, hath God said...?") as they undermine His Truth. Is God doing anything about it? Yes. As evidenced by what's been presented here and so much more, He is sending "strong delusion" among those who have not a "love of the truth" (2 Thessalonians 2:10,11).

We desperately need to heed the words of Jesus in Revelation chapters 2-3 that give critical warnings to churches that profess to be His. To Laodicea, which very likely represents the last church age before His return, He declares,

> As many as I love, I rebuke and chasten: be zealous therefore, and repent. Behold, I stand at the door, and knock: if any man hear my voice, and open the door, I will come in to him, and will sup with him, and he with me. To him that overcometh will I grant to sit with me in my throne, even as I also overcame, and am set down with my Father in his throne. He that hath an ear, let him hear what the Spirit saith unto the churches. (Revelation 3:19-22)

March 2008

6

THE SHAMEFUL SOCIAL GOSPEL

For I am not ashamed of the gospel of Christ:
for it is the power of God unto salvation
to every one that believeth.

— ROMANS 1:16 —

For various reasons, Christians of different sorts have tinkered with "the gospel of Christ" as though it needed adjustments. Not major alterations, most will tell you, but just some minor tweaking here and there. The changes often begin by one's declaring that there is no real change involved, simply a shift in emphasis. Yet, no matter what the rationale may be, the end result is being "ashamed of the gospel of Christ."

To be "ashamed of the gospel" covers a number of attitudes from being totally embarrassed by it to thinking one can improve upon it a bit to make it more acceptable. One example of the former is the recent claim by an Emerging Church author that the teaching regarding Christ's paying the full penalty for the sins of mankind through His substitutionary death on the Cross is irrelevant and viewed as "a form of cosmic child abuse." More subtle examples include trying to make the gospel seem less exclusive, and the "softening" of the consequences from which the gospel saves mankind, such as the wrath of God and the Lake of Fire.

Prevalent among many religious leaders who profess to be evangelical Christians (i.e., Bible-believing Christians) is the promotion of a gospel that is acceptable to, and even admired by, people throughout the world. Today, the most popular form of this is the social gospel.

Although the social gospel is common to many new movements among evangelicals, it is not new to Christendom. It had its modern beginning in the late 1800s, when it developed as a way to address the various conditions in society that caused suffering among the populace. The belief was, and is, that Christianity will attract followers when it demonstrates its love for mankind. This could be best accomplished by helping to alleviate the suffering of humanity caused by poverty, disease, oppressive work conditions, society's injustices, civil rights abuses, etc. Those who fostered this movement also believed that relief from their conditions of misery would improve the moral nature of those so deprived.

Another driving force behind the introduction of the social gospel was the eschatological, or end times, views of those involved. Nearly all were amillennialists or post-millennialists. The former believed that they were living in a (symbolic thousand-year) time period in which Christ was ruling from heaven, Satan was bound, and they were God's workers appointed to bring about a kingdom on earth worthy of Christ. Post-millennialists also believed they were in the Millennium, and their goal was to restore the earth to its Eden-like state in order for Christ to return from heaven to rule over His earthly kingdom.

The social gospel, in all of its assorted applications, helped to produce some achievements (child labor laws and women's suffrage) that have contributed to the welfare of society. It became the primary gospel of liberal theologians and mainline denominations throughout the 20th century. Although its popularity alternately rose and fell as it ran its course, it was often energized by the combination of religion and liberal politics, e.g., Martin Luther King Jr. and the civil rights movement. Midway through the last century and later, the social gospel influenced developments such as the liberation theology of Roman Catholicism and the socialism of left-leaning evangelical Christians. It is in this present century, however, that the social gospel has gotten its most extensive promotion. Two men, both professing to be evangelicals, have led the way.

George W. Bush began his presidency by instituting the White House Office of Faith-Based and Community Initiatives. His objective was to provide government funding for local churches, synagogues, mosques, and other religious ministries that were providing a social service to their community. Bush believed that programs run by "people of faith" could be at least as effective as secular organizations in helping the needy, and perhaps more so because of their moral commitment to "love and serve their neighbor." As he prepared to leave office, he declared that he considered his Faith-Based program to be one of the foremost achievements in his tenure as president. Presidential candidate Barack Obama stated that, should he win the election, he would continue the Faith-Based and Community Initiatives.

Rick Warren, the mega-selling author of *The Purpose-Driven Church* and *The Purpose-Driven Life*, has taken the social gospel to where it's never been before: not only worldwide but into the thinking and planning of world leaders. Warren credits business management genius Peter Drucker with the basic concept that he is executing. Drucker believed that the social problems of poverty, disease, hunger, and ignorance were beyond the capability of governments or multinational corporations to solve. To Drucker, the most hopeful solution would be found in the nonprofit sector of society, especially churches, with their hosts of volunteers dedicated to alleviating the social ills of those in their community.

Warren, acknowledging the late Drucker as his mentor for 20 years, certainly learned his lessons. His two *Purpose-Driven* books, translated into 57 languages and selling a combined 30 million copies, reveal the game plan for what Drucker had envisioned. Warren had local churches implement this vision from his books through his enormously popular 40 Days of Purpose and 40 Days of Community programs. To date, 500,000 churches in 162 nations have become part of his network. They form the basis for his Global P.E.A.C.E. Plan.

What is his P.E.A.C.E. plan? Warren's presentation of the plan to the church is found at www.thepeaceplan.com. On video, he identifies the "giants" of humanity's ills as spiritual emptiness, self-centered leadership, poverty, disease, and illiteracy, which he hopes to eradicate by (P)lanting churches, (E)quipping leaders, (A)ssisting the poor, (C)aring for the sick, and (E)ducating the next generation.

Warren uses the analogy of a three-legged stool to illustrate the best way to slay these giants. Two of the legs are governments and business, which have thus far been ineffective, and, just like a two-legged stool, cannot stand. The third very necessary leg is the church. "There are thousands of villages in the world that have no school, no clinic, no business, no government—but they have a church. What would happen if we could mobilize churches to address those five global giants?" Warren reasons that since there are 2.3 billion Christians worldwide, they could potentially form what President Bush has termed a vast "army of compassion" of "people of faith" such as the world has not yet experienced.

In addition to the *Christian version*, Warren has an expanded *inclusive version* of the P.E.A.C.E. plan that has drawn support and praise from political and religious leaders and celebrities worldwide. At the 2008 World Economic Forum, he declared, "The future of the world is not secularism, but religious pluralism...." Referring to the ills besetting the world, he declared, "We cannot solve these problems without involving people of faith and their religious institutions. It isn't going to happen any other way. On this planet there are about 20 million Jews, there are about 600 million Buddhists, there are about 800 million Hindus, there are over 1 billion Muslims, and there are 2.3 billion Christians. If you take people of faith out of the equation, you have ruled out five-sixths of the world. And if we only leave it up to secular people to solve these major problems, it isn't going to happen" (http://www. youtube.com/ watch?v=rGytW4yh0C8).

To accommodate working with people of all faiths Warren has revised the "P" in his P.E.A.C.E. from "planting evangelical churches" to "(P)romoting reconciliation" and the "E" from "equipping [church] leaders" to "(E)quipping ethical leaders." Warren has elsewhere acknowledged his practical shift to pluralism: "Who's the man of peace in any village—or it might be a woman of peace—who has the most respect?...They don't have to be Christian. In fact, they could be Muslim, but they're open and they're influential, and you work with them to attack the five giants [to which he has added global warming]." He quotes a secular leader who affirms what he's doing: "I get it, Rick. Houses of worship are the distribution centers for all we need to do."

Warren has joined the advisory board of Faith Foundation, established by former British prime minister and recent Roman Catholic convert Tony Blair. The Foundation's goal is to further understanding and cooperation among the six leading faiths: Christian, Muslim, Hindu, Buddhist, Sikh, and Jewish. How does the Cross fit into this ecumenical gathering? It doesn't. Critical to achieving that ecumenical goal is the elimination of the problem of *exclusive* religions, a concern articulated by one of the World Economic Forum panelists: "There are some religious leaders in different religious faiths who, in seeking to affirm their own faith and its authenticity and legitimacy...deny other people their faith with its legitimacy and authenticity. I don't think we can keep going like this without...spawning the kind of hatred we are all here to try and solve. I think it's up to us to hold the clergy's feet to the fire of whatever faith. That we insist that we affirm what is beautiful in our own traditions while at the same time refusing to denigrate other faith traditions by suggesting that they are illegitimate, or consigned to some kind of evil end."

The Bible declares all the religions of the world to be "illegitimate" and "consigned" not to "some kind of evil end" but to their *just* end. Only belief in the biblical gospel saves humanity: "Neither is there salvation in any other: for there is none other name [Jesus Christ] under heaven given among men, whereby we must be saved;...He that believeth on the Son hath everlasting life: and he that believeth not the Son shall not see life; but the wrath of God abideth on him" (Acts 4:12; John 3:36).

The history of the social gospel is, in nearly every case, a sincere attempt by Christians to do those things that they believe will honor God and benefit humanity. In every case, however, the practical working out of "benefiting humanity" has compromised biblical faith and dishonored God. Why is that? God's Word gives no commission to the church to fix the problems of the world. Those who attempt to do so are starting out under a false premise, "...a way which seemeth right unto *a man*," not *God's* way. So where can it go from there? "The end thereof are the ways of death," i.e., destruction (Proverbs 14:12). Furthermore, the problems of the world are all *symptoms*. The root cause is sin.

What percentage of the "people of faith," who comprise all religions and make up five-sixths of the world's population, understand and accept the gospel—the only cure for sin? Or how many of the 2.3 billion "Christians" in the world believe the biblical gospel? The numbers tumble down exponentially.

"Yes, but…they are a massive volunteer force and distribution outlet of resources for slaying the giants of world suffering!" What does it profit the billions of "people of faith" who may alleviate some of the world's symptoms yet lose their very souls?

The social gospel is a deadly disease for "people of faith." It reinforces the belief that salvation can be attained by doing good works, putting aside differences for the common good, treating others the way we want to be treated, acting morally, ethically, and sacrificially—and that doing so will endear humans to God. No. These are self-deceptive strivings that spurn God's salvation, deny His perfect standard, and reject His perfect justice. Salvation is "not of works, lest any man should boast." In fact, it is "by grace are ye saved through faith; and that not of yourselves: it is the gift of God"(Ephesians 2:8,9). Jesus declared Himself to be condemned humanity's only hope for reconciliation with God: "I am the way, the truth, and the life: no man cometh unto the Father, but by me" (John 14:6). There is no other way, because God's perfect justice demanded that the penalty for sin for every human ("for all have sinned"– Romans 3:23) be paid. Only the perfect, sinless God-Man could and did pay that infinite penalty in full by His death upon the Cross. Only faith in Him reconciles a person with God.

The shameful social gospel today not only promotes "another gospel," it helps prepare a kingdom contrary to the teachings of Scripture. "For our conversation [citizenship] is in heaven; from whence also we look for the Savior, the Lord Jesus Christ" (Philippians 3:20). He will return from heaven (John 14:3) to "rapture," or catch, those who believe in Him (His bride) up into the clouds and take them to heaven (1 Thessalonians 4:17).

The kingdom that remains on the earth will be the kingdom of the Antichrist.

Consistent with its amillennial/postmillennial beginnings, the efforts of the social gospel are earthbound in their attempted restoration of the kingdom of God. Eugene Peterson has infiltrated that heresy into his *Message* Bible: "God didn't go to all the trouble of sending his Son merely to point an accusing finger, telling the world how bad it was. He came to help, to put the world right again" (a perversion of John 3:17).

Rob Bell, in his book *Velvet Elvis*, reflects the "fix the earth" eschatology of nearly all Emerging Church leaders: "Salvation is the entire universe being brought back into harmony with its maker. This has huge implications for how people present the message of Jesus. Yes, Jesus can come into our hearts. But we can join a movement that is as wide and as big as the universe itself. Rocks and trees and birds and swamps and ecosystems. God's desire is to restore all of it....The goal isn't escaping this world but making this world the kind of place God can come to. And God is remaking us into the kind of people who can do this kind of work."

For Emerging Church leader Brian McLaren, this is the future way of life for the Christian. In an interview July 28, 2008, on *ChristianPost.com*, he said: "I think our future will also require us to join humbly and charitably with people of other faiths—Muslim, Hindu, Buddhist, Jewish, secularists, and others—in pursuit of peace, environmental stewardship, and justice for all people, things that matter greatly to the heart of God." No, what matters to the "heart of God" is "that all should come to repentance" and believe the gospel.

Anyone who puts his hope in this social gospel, which employs "people of faith" to make "this world the kind of place God can come to," needs to heed the words of Jesus in Luke 18:8: "When the Son of man cometh, shall he find faith on the earth?" People of *all faiths*, yes, but certainly not "*the* faith," for which Jude exhorts true believers to earnestly contend. Lord, help us all not to be ashamed of Your gospel!

September 2008

7

THE "JESUS" THE WORLD LOVES

I am come in my Father's name, and ye receive me not:
if another shall come in his own name,
him ye will receive.

— JOHN 5:43 —

What do you think of Jesus? That's a question I've asked at times to engage non-Christians in conversation about Him for the purpose of witnessing. A fairly typical response used to be that He was a religious teacher who did a lot of good, said many good things, and they usually concluded with a belief that He was a very good man. I then could ask, "Did you know that He claimed to be God?" When looks of puzzlement followed, I would explain that He couldn't be a "very good man." In claiming to be God, He was either self-deluded or an outright fraud—that is, unless He was telling the truth. More often than not, that thought, raising the issue of being accountable to God, would bring our conversation to an awkward end. At least it had provided the opportunity to plant some seeds that I hoped would grow into conviction. Most people aren't comfortable with the truth about Jesus.

Those who *profess* to be Christians quite often have ideas about Jesus that are just as wrong as those people who are not Christians. For example, Jehovah's Witnesses believe that Jesus is a created god and that He is also Michael the Archangel. Mormons believe Jesus is the spirit brother of Lucifer and that He was married and had children. The followers of Christian Science and the Religious Science religions believe that Jesus was simply a man upon whom the "Christ empowerment" came. Roman Catholics believe that the bread and wine of the Eucharist can be transubstantiated, or changed, into the literal body and blood of Jesus, who is then ingested into one's stomach. Lutherans believe that Jesus is *con*substantiated, or present, "in, with, and under" the bread and wine of communion. Such unbiblical beliefs are a mere handful among hundreds promoted by various Christian denominations and cults. Yet what is even more appalling is that an inquiry about Jesus today among those who call themselves evangelicals (Bible-believing Christians!) too often reveals "another Jesus" and a "false Christ." How does that happen?

Let's start with how one comes to a true knowledge of, and relationship with, Jesus Christ. It begins with a simple understanding of the gospel[1] that Jesus is God,[2] who became a Man[3] in order to save mankind from everlasting separation from God[4] that resulted from man's sin.[5] Jesus satisfied the perfect justice of God[6] by His once-and-for-all payment for the sins of humanity[7] through His death on the Cross.[8] His resurrection from the dead[9] assures the salvation of all those who acknowledge before God their sin[10] and their hopelessness in saving themselves,[11] and who by grace through faith[12] accept Christ's sacrifice on their behalf[13] and His free gift of eternal life.[14] This is how one is reconciled to God[15] and born again spiritually.[16] This is how one's relationship with the biblical Jesus Christ[17] begins.

Although that relationship is supernatural in that every true believer in Christ is indwelt by God,[18] it nevertheless progresses, as any good relationship does, by getting to know the person with whom one has a relationship.

The primary way a relationship with Jesus develops is by reading the revelation of Himself given in His Word. This is the only way to obtain specific information about Him that is objective and absolutely true. In addition, not only is the content of Scripture inspired by the Holy Spirit,[19] but that same Spirit of Truth is given to believers to understand that content.[20] How then could those who profess to follow God's Word come up with erroneous ideas about Jesus? Regrettably, many are getting their information about Jesus from sources outside the Bible or second hand from those who claim to be teaching what the Bible says about our Lord.

To demonstrate how ludicrous a relationship dependent upon such sources of knowledge is, consider what might happen to a husband and wife who try to form an intimate relationship with each other by relying on the insights of other people who claim to know them. That's a sure recipe for failure, yet Christians often run to extrabiblical sources for their knowledge of Jesus.

The amazing popularity of the book *The Shack* among evangelicals is just a recent example of someone depicting a Jesus who is foreign to the Bible and worse. What does the author think about Jesus? He characterizes Him in a way that may make some people feel more comfortable with Him, yet the Jesus of *The Shack* is clearly a false Christ. He's a "good old boy," who likes to fix things and takes "pleasure in cooking and gardening." He laughs at crude jokes, is a bit of a klutz, engages in trout fishing by chasing one down as He runs on water, carves a coffin for the body of a little girl, and enjoys kissing, hugging, and laughing with the two other members of the "Trinity." The book is filled with dialogue from the characters of God the Father (portrayed as an overweight Afro-American woman), the Holy Spirit (a petite Asian woman), and Jesus. All three speak as the "oracles of God," giving insights and explanations neither found in nor consistent with Scripture. Some enthusiastic readers say the words and interactions with the Godhead have comforted them, answered difficult questions about their faith, and made the person of the Lord seem all the more real to them.

The reality is that out of his own imagination the author has put *his* words into the mouths of Father, Son, and Holy Spirit, which are then perceived by multitudes as "thus saith the Lord." This is not only a bogus secondhand source but the arrogance of false prophecy at least and blasphemy and idolatry at worst. It is man, making God in his own *fallen* image.

More influential among evangelicals than *The Shack* is Mel Gibson's *The Passion of the Christ*, which became a huge box-office success, thanks mostly to evangelical support. Available now as a "definitive edition DVD," it features, for those who want the official Catholic theology of the film explained, a discussion with director Mel Gibson, along with a Catholic apologist and two Catholic priests who were the film's theological consultants. The movie has a false gospel, a false Christ, and is loaded with supposedly biblical scenes from the minds of Gibson and a Catholic nun given to mystical hallucinations. Yet it continues to be used extensively by evangelical churches, especially during Lent and Easter week.

In response to "What do you think of Jesus?" millions who saw the movie now mistakenly believe that: He was confronted by Satan in the Garden of Gethsemane; He was thrown from a bridge by His captors and dangled from a chain; His image was captured for posterity on the veil of a woman named Veronica; as His cross began to fall, it levitated to keep Him from hitting the ground, and, most contradictory to the gospel, it was the merciless scourging He suffered that paid for the sins of humanity.

These are only a few of the unbiblical images that the world and many in the church have added to their perception of Jesus. Movies are today's most popular form of disseminating superficial information and misinformation. Feature films about Jesus and God have put erroneous ideas about them into the hearts and minds of the masses: *Jesus Christ Superstar; The Last Temptation of Christ; Bruce Almighty; The Da Vinci Code; Judas; Oh God!; Oh God, Book II; Jesus of Nazareth*, to name but a few.

What about "more biblically accurate" Bible movies— those that take the words directly from Scripture, for example?

When you have an actor portraying Jesus who says only the words of Jesus that are found in the Bible, does that make the portrayal more accurate? More accurate than what? Does the actor actually *look* like Jesus, or *talk* like Jesus, or *reflect the godly demeanor* of Jesus? More critically, can he accurately imitate the God-Man, the Creator of the Universe, the One in whom all things consist? Even if he could, which is impossible, it would still be an imitation! Furthermore, he will leave millions, including believers, with an image of a false "Christ."

A few such movies are sincere attempts at communicating the content and stories of the Scriptures through *visual media*. Although sincere, they are doomed to failure regarding truth. Why? In addition to what was noted above, the Bible is an objective revelation from God given in words. All attempts at visually translating those words abandon objective revelation in favor of subjective interpretation. Take a passage of Scripture, for instance, and have five people give their understanding of the verse based upon the context, the grammatical structure, and the normal meaning of the words. More often than not, the interpretations will be quite similar. Should one of the five come up with something very different, it can be corrected by simply checking it out objectively against the context, grammar, and accepted definitions of the words in the passage. On the other hand, what if five artists were to translate the passage visually? The result would be five very subjective and quite different renderings. Even if only one artist visually translated the verse and four people tried to interpret the image, you would likely have four different views because the medium has no objective criteria comparable to that of words. Are you getting the "picture" here? Imagery is not the way to communicate objective truth.

God did not draw pictures on the tablets He gave to Moses. His continual command to him and to His other prophets was to *write down His instructions*. Visual imagery was at the heart of pagan worship used by people whose lives centered around idols—the chief by-product being unbridled superstition. The same was true of the medieval Roman Catholic and Orthodox Churches, who fed their followers images rather than teaching them to read and write (as the Jews had done successfully from the time of Abraham). Even today, superstition continues to be rampant within those visually oriented religious systems.

Where does the world get its ideas about Jesus? Most non-Christians only know what they've picked up from sources they regard as Christian, although rarely is the content biblical. More than a billion Muslims, for example, hold a view of Jesus that Muhammad gleaned from questionable Christians. The Qur'an states that Isa (Jesus) is not the Son of God because Allah has no son. Isa's birth took place under a palm tree, and, while still a babe, he cried out from his cradle that he was a servant of Allah, who had given him a revelation and made him a prophet. He did not die upon the cross; someone took his place—all in contradiction to the Bible.

Many Jews put stock in the alleged Talmudic stories that oppose the gospel accounts. They have been taught that Jesus was an illegitimate child who was born to a harlot and a scoundrel. Declaring himself to be the Messiah, he performed healings by sorcery and consequently was stoned and then hung on a tree for his magic and blasphemy for claiming to be the Son of God.

Hindus have added Jesus as one more avatar, or god, among their 330 million gods. All of their gurus who have become popular in the West—from Maharishi Mahesh Yogi to Rajneesh—preach their own "Jesus." Buddhists, such as the 14th Dalai Lama, regard Jesus as a *bodhisattva*, or enlightened god, among multitudes of gods reincarnated for the service of humanity.

Incredibly, the above erroneous beliefs about Jesus are fostered within professing Christianity by a popular practice among Emerging Church fellowships. Some invite the followers of the world religions for "conversation" in order to learn more about Jesus from a pluralistic perspective. The goal seems to be to establish a Jesus who is acceptable to people of all faiths—or no faith. A common refrain heard from the Emergent communities is "We love Jesus but not His church." Certainly, as the church has compromised with the world, there is much not to like. Yet sadly, for many, it is neither the biblical Jesus whom they love nor the biblical church that they support. Some are under the delusion that Jesus is becoming more respected in our culture. That has never been the case for the Jesus revealed in Scripture.

It is hard for anyone who has a personal, intimate relationship with Jesus Christ to accept that the world hates Him, this One whom we love so much. It was difficult for me, and I still struggle with that. How could anyone reject the One who loves us more than we could ever comprehend, and whose sacrifice for those He created is so wonderfully unfathomable? Such hatred is often masked and develops progressively and by stealth. It is found in Satan's strategy that began with "Yea, hath

God said…?" His dialogue with Eve provided a ripe opportunity to subvert the truth about God and His command. Eve bought the Adversary's lying alteration of God's character and his denial of the consequence of disobedience. Her offspring down through the ages have done likewise.

Yet that reality in the guise of condescension and mockery nearly moved me to despair as I reviewed a particular episode of Fox TV's *The Family Guy*. The program (presented by the same network that created "Fox Faith" to market movies to Christian families) featured a Jesus character who left heaven to get away from his "nit-picking, overbearing father"; who proves his "deity" by changing meals into ice cream sundaes and enlarging a woman's breasts; who walks on water to fetch a five-dollar bill; who appears on *Jay Leno* and an MTV award show; who goes to Hollywood, gets drunk at a party, and lands in jail, and who comes to the conclusion that he's not mature enough yet to help the world. I immediately searched for protests from Christendom against this Fox TV top-rated program. There were found neither cries of outrage nor weeping for those who blasphemed and ridiculed the only One who could save them. Some Christians offered uneasy rationalizations that Jesus certainly must have a sense of humor. That's the Jesus the world wants.

My mind raced to the Garden of Gethsemane, thinking about our Savior on His knees in prayer before the Father, where in His anguish He sweat as it were great drops of blood. He would become sin for us. Our Creator would take our sins upon Himself and experience the eternal penalty due every soul. Although He would be triumphant in paying for the sins of mankind, He nevertheless cried out to the Father that if there was any other way to save humanity, to let this cup of separation pass. But there was no other way.

I thought of the Lord of Glory hanging upon the cross on Calvary's hill, with the mockers about Him. Yet He died for them— and for those who mock Him still.

Pray that we who truly know Him would not drift from Him because of "another Jesus" conjured up by the world, our own flesh, or the devil. Pray also that the Lord will enable us to reflect the true character of Christ in our words and deeds; that He will help us to show the world the true Jesus, who, being God, came in the likeness of man, was treated as though He were sin itself, and satisfied the divine justice of God by dying upon the Cross, thus providing salvation for all of mankind.

December 2008

8

Refashioning God

*Wherefore thou art great, O Lord God: for there is
none like thee, neither is there any God beside thee,
according to all that we have heard with our ears.*

— 2 Samuel 7:22 —

*And this is life eternal, that they might know thee the
only true God, and Jesus Christ, whom thou hast sent.*

— John 17:3 —

Every man, woman, and child has the opportunity to spend eternity with God. That's mind-boggling! There is nothing imaginable that could possibly be more exciting and wonderful. Moreover, that possibility isn't something that man has invented. From Genesis through the book of Revelation, the Scriptures declare and explain how that becomes a reality. It's what the Bible is all about.

In God's revelation of Himself through His Word, we learn of His attributes and personal qualities in the only way

that mankind can know Him accurately. Without His revelation, we are left with finite man's speculations and guesses
about an infinite God. Such guesswork is often the basis of all
the religions of the world. Their deities and their beliefs are the
product of the imagination of fallen humanity (with the help
of fallen angels). Biblical Christianity is the only exception.
God has declared Himself in very specific terms to mankind.
Without an accurate source of information, which only God
himself could and did provide, mankind would be left with
nothing more than mythology, and most of the world is mired
in this.

Tragically, a similar condition is infecting those who
profess to be biblical Christians; they are slipping into the
same swamp of delusion. That's one of the reasons why so
few Christians seem truly excited about eternity and spending
it with the Lord. They can't relate to it—or to Him—with
real confidence. Many are tossed to and fro by their thoughts
about God drawn from extra-biblical sources, from the latest
best-selling Christian books, to Christian television program-
ming, to what Oprah and her guests have conjured up. What's
being communicated about God is usually pleasing (albeit to
the flesh) but is rarely true to His holy character. Even the
most appealing ideas about God, when they don't ring true
to the Scriptures, contribute to a misleading and superficial
relationship with the One we are to love in truth and with all
our heart, soul, mind, and strength.

John, the beloved Apostle, tells us in his epistle that believers love God because He first loved us (1 John 4:19). That love for
Him began with a basic understanding of who He is and what

He has done for us. When we finally understood and believed the simple gospel (that God so loved us that He became a Man in order to reconcile us to Himself through His life, death, and resurrection), Jesus saved us. He did what only God could do—provided salvation for all mankind by paying the infinite penalty for sin that God's perfect justice required.

At our new birth in Christ, which begins each believer's personal relationship with Him, He gives us the Holy Spirit, the Spirit of Truth, to live within us, to teach us His Word, and to help us to grow in the knowledge of God our Savior. That's the only way we can truly know, and mature in our relationship with, Jesus. Anything that deviates from *God's* way of knowing Him is a delusion that leads down a slippery slope to destruction. In this day of quick fixes, running after instant gratification, and experiential catharses, we need to heed Isaiah's counsel regarding spiritual maturity: "Whom shall he teach knowledge? and whom shall he make to understand doctrine? them that are weaned from the milk, and drawn from the breasts. For precept must be upon precept, precept upon precept; line upon line, line upon line; here a little, and there a little" (Isaiah 28:9-10). These precepts are God's instructions, His full counsel, which are completely sufficient for His children. As Peter declared, "According as his divine power hath given unto us all things that pertain unto life and godliness, through the knowledge of him that hath called us to glory and virtue" (2 Peter 1:3). That's God's way of developing maturity and fruitfulness (not to mention confidence in and a greater love for Him!) among His saints: "For if these things be in you, and abound, they make you that ye shall neither be barren nor unfruitful in the knowledge of our Lord Jesus Christ" (2 Peter 1:8).

There is nothing complicated about God's plan. So, what's the problem? Each one of us has to ask himself or herself that question, whether indeed, we have not taken to heart, or have willfully deviated from, God's instructions. As Isaiah pointed out, the learning/maturing process is quite simple ("precept upon precept"), but it does require learning what the precepts are and a willingness to do them. I'm speaking to my own heart as much as anyone else's when it comes to whether or not I fall short of what God desires in all of this.

For thirty years prior to accepting Jesus as my Lord and Savior by faith alone, I had many beliefs about Him that were without support from the Scriptures—even contradictory. Some of the ideas came from the nuns and priests who, in many ways, were a wonderful part of my life growing up Catholic, whether in elementary school, private school, or high school. What they taught me was mostly unbiblical, including many things that were not even accepted as official Church dogma. The most notable example was the common belief that Jesus, for all practical and even eternal purposes, was subject to His mother, Mary. Her position as *Mater Dei*, the Mother of God (we were told), made her the most advantageous source of obtaining favors from Jesus. That certainly made sense to me and to the friends of my youth. After all, what good son would refuse his mom anything? Imagery of Christ as a small child with the Madonna was seemingly everywhere Catholic, from classic art and statuary to the many apparitions of Mary holding a baby—from the 1600s right up to the present, including

Medugorje and Egypt. No one I knew who had collected holy cards (a popular practice of Catholics of my generation) of the Infant Jesus of Prague, or St. Anthony, or St. Joseph holding the infant Jesus, gave any thought to the biblical fact that Jesus was in His early thirties when He ascended into heaven. Such things created an impression about Jesus that was endearing yet deadly in its straying from the truth about our all-knowing and all-powerful sovereign God.

The erroneous Catholic ideas about Jesus (that a piece of bread is changed into the body and blood of Jesus in the Eucharist, that He did not pay the full penalty for our sins, etc.,) may not seem too surprising to evangelicals because, as most know, the Church of Rome doesn't strictly adhere to the Bible. To that she has added Sacred Tradition and the Sacred Magisterium, through which the bishops claim to infallibly interpret Tradition and the Bible. What is tragic is that evangelicals, who traditionally have regarded the Bible alone as their authority in all matters of faith and practice, are increasingly turning to extrabiblical sources for their instruction regarding spiritual matters. That's not exactly new; popular Christian books have displaced the books of the Bible in many so-called Bible studies throughout the land. Multitudes seem to prefer the insights of Beth Moore, John Eldredge, and Max Lucado over the Holy Spirit-inspired prophets of Scripture. Sadly, man's opinions and subtle and not-so-subtle psychobabble have become the oracles of wisdom for most of Christianity.

For decades, because of the influence of psychology on the church, professing Christians have integrated psychotherapeutic concepts into the way they view themselves, as opposed to what the Bible teaches about humanity. For example, many if not most Christians, believe the humanistic concepts of self-esteem and self-love to be consistent with Scripture, although they are absolutely contrary to the Word of God. Why, then, are those concepts accepted by evangelicals? Primarily because Dr. James Dobson and a host of other influential Christian psychologists promote them. Man's ideas and pseudo-scientific speculations have become the so-called guiding light of increasing numbers of Christian families. Yet there is something even more ominous than the leaven of man's ways mixed with God's way in the life of a Christian. It amounts to refashioning one's view of God from a human perspective.

All of us, from time to time, have had thoughts about God that did not square exactly with what He himself has declared in the Scriptures, but that generation of misinformation has reached appalling levels among evangelical Christians today. This development has been stimulated primarily by the Church Growth and Emerging Church movements in their approach to allegedly reaching our culture for Christ. Reinventing Christ and Christianity, in order to make them more acceptable to the unsaved masses, is both the method and the goal. It amounts to recreating God in the fallen image of man. As delusionary as that approach may seem in attempting to reach the lost, astonishingly, it has millions of professing Christians caught in its web of deception.

Though many examples could be cited, the most popular vehicle of this tactic is a fictional book that has been atop the *New York Times* best-seller list for about 60 weeks, is available in 35 languages, and has sold more than seven million copies.

I'm referring to *The Shack* (mentioned in the previous chapter) by William Paul Young. Multitudes have claimed that the book has transformed their lives by giving them a "new and wonderful awareness about God that they never understood from the Bible." The story centers upon a man, Mack Philips, whose young daughter was abducted during a family vacation. Although her body hadn't been found, evidence pointing to her murder was discovered in an abandoned shack in the wilderness of Eastern Oregon; hence the title.

After several years, which have played emotional havoc with Mack and his family (he calls this time "The Great Sadness"), he receives a note in his mailbox inviting him back to the shack. The note is signed, "Papa," a very private and intimate name that Mack's wife affectionately uses for God. Mack apprehensively follows through with the invitation and encounters the godhead, Father, Son, and Holy Spirit, in ways, means, and manifestations that are both unbiblical and bizarre. God the Father appears as a stereotyped, overweight black woman, who, nevertheless, is called Papa. She's a bit crude at times, likes to boogie to funk music, and some of her dialogue makes you wonder if she got past the third grade: "Well, Mackenzie, don't just stand there gawkin' with your mouth open like your pants are full"; "Take it easy on those greens, young man. Those things can give you the trots if you ain't careful." And when asked if there was anyone in the world of whom she was *not* especially fond, she replies, "Nope, I haven't been able to find any. Guess that's jes' the way I is."

The book may be fiction, but God is not. If God the Father, God the Son, and God the Holy Spirit say and do things in this novel that are out of character with how they are revealed in Scripture, they are obviously false representations. Insights and explanations about God constitute doctrine. They are either true to God's Word, reflecting sound doctrine, or they are lies or fables that men concoct. Paul's prophetic words of warning in 2 Timothy 4:3-4 are evident in the popularity of *The Shack*: "For the time will come when they will not endure sound doctrine; but after their own lusts shall they heap to themselves teachers, having itching ears; And they shall turn away their ears from the truth, and shall be turned unto fables."

The Jesus character is a giggling "good ol' boy" who is enamored by His creation. A bit of a klutz, he drops a bowl of sauce that splatters all over Papa's skirt, giving the three persons of the "Trinity" a good laugh. When questioned by Mack about his less-than-good looks, Jesus blames it on his "big Jewish nose," which he says he got from Mary's side of the family, specifically his grandfather. We learn that Jesus likes to fish for trout by trying to chase them down as he runs on water. He has yet to be successful but thoroughly enjoys the sport. Referring to the female Papa's unexpected crudeness, he declares, "She's a riot." Throughout the story, Jesus can't seem to restrain his giggles and chuckles. He and the other persons of the Trinity are so like us that many readers claim they are now "more comfortable" with God. It's astonishing that what amounts to slandering the character of our holy God could make a professing Christian *comfortable*.

Nearly all of the literary devices in the book are either emotional or psychological hooks. The bait is "meeting felt needs." For example, Jesus the Carpenter constructs a coffin for the now-found body of Mack's daughter, although she makes her daddy feel better by communicating to him from heaven (necromancy?) that she's quite happy. As another example, the reason that God the Father appears as a woman to Mack is because he had a bad attitude toward his own dysfunctional father (who made it to heaven anyway, in keeping with the universalism [everyone is finally reconciled to God] implied in the novel). Heresies and distortions of biblical truth are found in page after page of *The Shack*.

Thinking of Jesus' words in Matthew 24 that false Christs would arise and lead many astray, the Jesus of *The Shack* readily qualifies as a fulfillment of that prophecy. Again, more than seven million people have thus far been presented a bogus Jesus, and, for some, that may be their one and only introduction to him. That grieves me deeply. A false Jesus can save no one. Erroneous ideas about Jesus will destroy any hope of a *truly fruitful* relationship with Him. Jesus was, and is, certainly human. But He is also God, and His humanity was and is perfect in every aspect. In that light, all attempts to make Him seem more like us—sinful humanity—either in a book or in our minds, is an act of blasphemy. Blasphemy isn't just bad-mouthing God or Jesus; it's attributing characteristics to Him that are not true—any false characteristics. It is conjuring up "another Jesus," which Scripture condemns.

"This I say therefore, and testify in the Lord, that ye henceforth walk not as other Gentiles walk, in the vanity of their mind, Having the understanding darkened, being alienated from the life of God through the ignorance that is in

them, because of the blindness of their heart" (Ephesians 4:17-18).
The success of *The Shack* among those who profess to be evangelicals is as shameful as it is destructive, yet it also indicates
that "vanity" of mind and "ignorance" are not the exclusive
domain of unbelievers. Only a love for the truth and a willingness to do what the Word of God says will preserve us from the
apostasy that Scripture tells us will overtake the world.

*Lord, help us to remain steadfast in the faith, submitting to
You in all things, and worshiping You in Spirit and in truth.
Maranatha!*

August 2009

9

THE WORKS-SALVATION DELUSION

I do not frustrate the grace of God: for if righteousness come[s] by the law, then Christ is dead in vain.

— GALATIANS 2:21 —

When we compare biblical Christianity with the religions of the world, using the Scriptures to guide us, we see that the gap between them is unbridgeable. In fact, one is forced to the conclusion that there are really only two religions in the world: biblical Christianity—and all other religions. (Note: I refer to biblical Christianity as a "religion" only for comparative purposes: a religion is a manmade belief system, whereas biblical Christianity is what God has revealed to mankind.)

These two "religions" are set apart primarily by what they teach about salvation—how one can get to heaven or paradise or Valhalla or Nirvana or the abode of God, or whatever else people believe about the afterlife. Each of the two can be placed under one of two categories: Human Achievement and Divine Accomplishment—or, to put it simply, the religions of "Do" and "Done." I'm referring to the fact that either there are things you must do (Human Achievement) or there is *nothing* you can do because it has already been done (Divine Accomplishment) to earn entrance to heaven.

Biblical Christianity alone comes under the heading of Divine Accomplishment. All the other religions of the world must be placed under the label of Human Achievement. Let's first consider some of the major religions, such as Hinduism, Buddhism, Islam, Judaism, and certain denominations or cults that profess to be Christian.

Hinduism has about 330 million gods who must be appeased through some type of ritual. A couple of years ago I was given a tour of a massive Hindu temple just outside Chicago. The parking lot was filled with luxury cars. There was imported stonework from Italy. No expense was spared. Inside, doctors, lawyers, and engineers, among others, according to my guide, were serving meals to the idols, Hanuman, the monkey god, and Ganesha, the elephant god.

Hinduism is a system of works—things that one must do to reach *moksha*, the Hindu heaven. It involves the practice of yoga, which, contrary to what many have heard, has never been for improvement of one's health but is rather a means of dying to one's body in the hope of delivering oneself from the physical realm. This is supposed to yoke one to Brahman, the Supreme Deity of Hinduism. Reincarnation, a system that supposedly enables one to work one's way to heaven through many births, deaths, and rebirths, is one of the teachings of this religion.

Buddhism is also all about works. Buddha believed that the key to reaching Nirvana, which is allegedly the state of perfect peace and happiness, is through an understanding of the Four Noble Truths and by practicing the Noble Eightfold Path.

In essence, the Four Noble Truths declare that we endure suffering because of our desires or cravings. These "Truths" claim that suffering will stop when we cease trying to fulfill those desires. According to Buddhism, we can achieve this by following the Noble Eightfold Path, which has the elements of "right view, right intention, right speech, right action, right livelihood, right effort, right mindfulness, and right concentration." This is all done by man's *achievement*, i.e., "doing things right" in order to reach Nirvana.

In Islam, paradise is attained when Allah weighs a follower's good works against his bad deeds on a scale at Judgment Day. The Qur'an declares: "For those things that are good remove those that are evil" (Surah 11:114). It's a quantitative process. Good deeds need to outweigh or blot out evil deeds. From the Qur'an again: "The balance that day will be true: Those whose scale [of good works] will be heavy, will prosper: Those whose scale will be light will find their souls in perdition" (Surah 7:8,9).

Here's an interesting example of what a Muslim faces to get into paradise: On April 3, 1991, the Egyptian magazine, *Akher Saa*, recorded a heated debate between four female journalists and Sheik Doctor Abdu-Almonim Al-Nimr, who holds a high position at Al-Azher Islamic University. One of the journalists asked him: "Is the *hijab* [veil or head covering] obligatory for women in Islam? If I do not wear the hijab, shall

I go to hell in spite of my other good deeds? I am talking about the decent woman who does not wear the hijab."

Dr. Al-Nimr replied, "The ordinances in Islam are many, my daughter, Allah made us accountable to each. It means if you do that ordinance you earn a point. If you neglect one, you lose a point. If you pray, you earn a point; if you do not fast you lose a point, and so on." He continued, "I did not invent a new theory...for every man there is a book in which all his good and evil deeds are recorded...even how do we treat our children."

The journalist said: "That means, if I do not wear the hijab, I will not enter the hell fire without taking into account the rest of my good deeds." Dr. Al-Nimr replied: "My daughter, no one knows who will enter the hell fire...I might be the first one to enter it. Caliph Abu-Bakr Al-Sadik said: 'I have no trust concerning Allah's schemes, even if one of my feet is inside of paradise who can determine which deed is acceptable and which is not.' *You do all that you can do*...and the accountability is with Allah. You ask him for acceptance [Italics added for emphasis]."

In Judaism, heaven is attained by keeping the Law and its ceremonies. Obviously, that isn't consistent with what the *Tanakh* (the Old Testament) teaches, yet that has been the practice of Judaism for millennia. As Jesus said, "In vain they do worship [God], teaching for doctrines the commandments of men" (Matthew 15:9).

His words also apply to a number of "Christian" denominations and cults that stress works as necessary for salvation. Jehovah's Witnesses, Mormons, Seventh-Day Adventists, the

Church of Christ adherents, Roman Catholics, Eastern and Russian Orthodox members, Lutherans, and many others all include something that needs to be accomplished or is necessary for salvation, whether it's baptism, the sacraments, or joining their particular organization and fulfilling their requirements.

Here is an example from the first 30 years of my own life as a Roman Catholic. I lived by a religious system of laws, many of which a Catholic is obligated to keep. It began with baptism. If one is not baptized, the Church says he can't enter heaven. It also says that although baptism is required, it is *no guarantee*. There are many other such rules that a Catholic *must* keep.

I have a book in my office called the *Code of Canon Law*. It contains 1,752 laws, many of which affect one's eternal destiny. Sins recognized by the Roman Catholic Church are classified as either mortal or venial. A mortal sin is one that damns a person to hell, should he or she die without having had it absolved by a priest. A venial sin doesn't need to be confessed to a priest, but whether confessed or not, all sin adds to one's temporal punishment, which must be expiated either here on earth through suffering or good works or else be purged in the flames of purgatory after one's death.

There are obligations that a Catholic must fulfill regarding both beliefs and deeds. For example, one is required to believe that Mary was conceived without sin (an event called the Immaculate Conception). If a Catholic doesn't believe that, he commits a mortal sin, which carries the penalty of eternal damnation. The feast day of the Immaculate Conception is a holy day of obligation, a day on which all Catholics are *required* to attend Mass. Failure to do so could result in commission of a mortal sin.

All the belief systems that I've mentioned, and many others as well, consist of doing or not doing certain things to reach "heaven." All are based upon human achievement. But what about biblical Christianity? How is that different?

Ephesians 2:8-9 spells it out for us: "For by grace are ye saved *through faith*; and that [salvation is] not of yourselves: it is the *gift* of God: *not of works*, lest any man should boast [emphasis added]." That's pretty straightforward. Our salvation doesn't have anything to do with our *achievements*.

Verse 8 tells us that it is by *grace* that we are saved. Grace is unmerited favor. If any merit is involved, it cannot be by grace. It's the gift of God. So if it's a gift, it can't be of works. That should be obvious. Someone puts in a tough month of work and his employer comes to him with his paycheck and declares, "Good job, Joe, here's your gift!" No—Joe *worked* for what he was paid. No gift was involved.

Regarding a person who works, Romans 4:4 tells us that his wages are a payment for the debt his employer owes him, and his paycheck has nothing to do with grace or a gift. A worker who has done a good job can boast or feel a sense of pride in the work he has accomplished. Yet all of that is contrary to grace or a gift. Grace rules out any sense of merit, and a gift does away with any sense of something earned or paid for.

Paul's teaching in Ephesians is affirmed in his epistle to Titus, chapter 3, verse 4:

> But after that the kindness and love of God our
> Saviour toward man appeared, *not by works* of
> righteousness which we have done, but according
> to his mercy he saved us, by the washing of regen-
> eration, and renewing of the Holy Ghost; which
> he shed on us abundantly through Jesus Christ
> our Saviour; that being justified by his grace, we
> should be made heirs according to the hope of
> eternal life. [Emphasis added]

We can see that this is consistent with Ephesians 2:8-9.
It's not by our *works* that we are saved—not by works of righteousness that we have *done*—but it's *by His mercy* that we are
saved.

You may well imagine that, as a Roman Catholic conditioned by a life of Church rules and rituals, I had great
difficulty believing that *faith* was the only basis by which I
could enter heaven. It didn't make sense to me.

Well, not only does it make sense—it's the only possible
way anyone can be saved. It is *miraculously sensible!*

First of all, what keeps anyone from heaven or eternal life
with God? We know that the answer is "sin." Here is a small
sampling of the applicable verses: All have sinned (Romans 3:23);
the wages of sin is death (Romans 6:23); sin separates us from God
(Isaiah 59:2); the soul who sins shall die (Ezekiel 18:20); sin brings
forth death (James 1:15).

In Genesis 2, God explains to Adam the consequences
of disobeying Him. Adam was told not to eat from a certain
fruit in the Garden of Eden. It was a commandment that was
related to obedience and love—not of God's withholding

something from Adam, as the Serpent implied. Remember, Jesus said "If a man love me, he will keep my words," that is, His teachings (John 14:23). Our love for God is demonstrated by our obedience.

What was God's penalty for disobedience? Genesis 2:17: "...for in the day that thou eatest thereof thou shalt surely die." Adam and Eve loved themselves more than they loved God, because they didn't "keep [His] words." They disobeyed Him, and the consequence was death. "The day you eat of it you will surely die." In the Scriptures, death always involves separation, and in God's judgment upon them, two applications are found: 1) physical death (the degeneration of the body, leading ultimately to its separation from the soul and spirit), and 2) eternal separation from God.

Adam and Eve did not die instantly, but the death process began at that point for them and for all creation. However, their *spiritual* relationship with God changed immediately and forever. God's judgment for sin is eternal: separation from God *forever*. It's an infinite penalty. And God, who is perfect in all of His attributes, including justice, had to carry out the punishment. He couldn't let them slide by and just give them another chance. That would have meant that He was not perfectly true to His Word. The penalty had to be paid.

So what could Adam and Eve do? Nothing, except die physically and spiritually, which is to be separated from God forever. And what can the rest of mankind do, seeing that *all have sinned*? Nothing. Well, one might ask, what if we do all sorts of good deeds that might outweigh our sins, or if we go to church a lot, or get baptized, do religious things, receive the sacraments, and so forth? None of those things will help us. Why? Because they don't pay the penalty. So what can we do? There is nothing that we *can* do—except to pay the penalty ourselves by being separated from God forever.

Our situation would be absolutely hopeless except that God has some other attributes in addition to being perfectly just. He is also perfect in love and mercy! "For God so loved the world" that He sent His only begotten Son to pay the penalty for us (John 3:16).

And that is exactly what Jesus did on the Cross. It is incomprehensible to us that during those three hours of darkness (when He cried out "My God, my God, why hast thou forsaken me?") He took on the sins of the world and suffered the wrath of His Father—for us. On the Cross He "tasted death for every man" (Hebrews 2:9), that is, He experienced and paid the infinite penalty for everyone's sins.

When that *divine accomplishment* ended, Jesus cried out, "It is finished," meaning that the penalty had been paid in full. It was a *divine* accomplishment because it was something that only God could do! God became a man and died physically, because physical death was part of the penalty. Yet, as the God-Man, he was able to experience fully the penalty that every sinner would experience—being spiritually separated from God forever.

God's justice demands payment. Either we pay the penalty ourselves or we turn to Jesus by faith and receive the benefits of His sacrificial atonement. What does Roman 6:23 say? "For the wages of sin is death; but the *gift* of God is eternal life through Jesus Christ our Lord." The Bible could not be more clear that salvation can only be "the gift of God" and that we can only appropriate that gift by faith.

Any attempt to merit salvation by our works is not only futile—it is impossible: "For whosoever shall keep the whole law, and yet offend in one point, he is guilty of all" (James 2:10). Worse yet, it is a denial of the infinite penalty that God imposed, a rejection of God's "unspeakable gift," and a repudiation of what Christ accomplished for us.

It used to be that most evangelicals would agree. This is no longer the case as the apostasy gathers momentum in these Last Days. Recently, a Pew Forum survey of more than 40,000 Americans found that 57 percent of those who said they were evangelicals believed that Jesus is not the exclusive way to heaven. Since Jesus is the only one who provides divine accomplishment, all that remains is the futile delusion of human achievement for salvation.

June 2010

10

WHAT'S YOUR "AFFECTION DIRECTION"?

If ye then be risen with Christ, seek those things which are above, where Christ sitteth on the right hand of God. Set your affection on things above, not on things on the earth. For ye are dead, and your life is hid with Christ in God. When Christ, who is our life, shall appear, then shall ye also appear with him in glory.

— COLOSSIANS 3:1-4 —

I'm fascinated by timelines. They give me an idea of what events took place in history, how they relate timewise to other historical events, and whether or not former events may have influenced later ones. I especially like biblical timelines. They often begin with the event of creation and end with the future Millennial reign of Jesus Christ from Jerusalem, supplying a host of details in between. Due to their temporal nature, however, they can only hint at eternity, which is infinite, and for which our life on earth is only a preparation.

Why am I making an issue of this? Because the world and, sadly, much of the church are caught up in a *temporal* delusion: clinging to this earth rather than hoping for heaven. It's part of Satan's strategy to deceive the world into building his kingdom. For thousands of years, he has seduced both professing and true Christians into joining his labor force, with the goal of establishing his own religion, which will be headed by his puppet ruler, the Antichrist. As the intensity of his program increases in these last days, particularly in Christendom, the leaven of this apostasy has been deposited in all theological camps: charismatics, Calvinists, conservatives, liberals, Pentecostals, Baptists, left-leaning Christians, supporters of the Emerging Church Movement, promoters of the "social gospel," et al.

In its simplest form, it is an attitude of disdaining what Paul admonishes us to do in Colossians 3:2: "Set your affection on things above, not on things on the earth." Although even those who truly know and love Jesus may struggle sometimes with keeping their affections on Him, there are others who profess Christ and claim to follow His Word yet who continue in their attempts to set up His kingdom here on earth prior to His return. That unbiblical objective, sometimes referred to as Dominion Theology and Kingdom-Dominionism, has taken many forms throughout church history.

One early example was the Holy Roman Empire. The idea was that "godly" (i.e., in support of the papacy) emperors would bring the world into the fold of Christ. When that wasn't successful, the papacy took control, ruling over most of the world at that time. As one historian describes it: "[The

Church of Rome governed the medieval world and] had all the apparatus of the state: laws and law courts, taxes and tax-collectors, a great administrative machine, power of life and death over the citizens of Christendom and their enemies within and without....Popes claimed the sole right of initiating and directing wars against unbelievers. They raised armies, conducted campaigns, and made treaties of peace in defense of their territorial interests."[1] Like most of the dogmas and practices of the Roman Catholic Church, this was contrary to what Jesus taught: "My kingdom is not of this world: if my kingdom were of this world, then would my servants fight... but now is my kingdom not from hence."

Amillennialism was the theological belief of the age, which posited that the Millennial, or 1,000-year, reign of Christ was already taking place, albeit spiritually. The worldly successes of the Roman Catholic Church seemed to support this view, but before long it succumbed to its own excesses and corruption. Although the Reformation was a reaction against the abuses of Catholicism, the Reformers kept the Catholic amillennial eschatology, along with many of its teachings and practices such as infant baptism and replacement theology (the belief that the church has replaced Israel). Verses from Scripture that spoke of blessings for Israel were spiritualized to denote the church; verses regarding Israel's punishment were ignored.

John Calvin attempted to make the city of Geneva a model of the kingdom of God, and, for his controlling effort, earned the title "the Protestant Pope." Although his goal was admirable, the results of his implementation were little different from what he had objected to in the Roman Catholic

Church. Historian Will Durant writes, "The new clergy… became under Calvin more powerful than any priesthood since Israel. The real law of a Christian state, said Calvin, must be the Bible, the clergy are the interpreters of that law, civil governments are subject to that law, and must enforce it as so interpreted."[2]

Another historian writes, "In a class by themselves stood crimes against Calvin. It was a crime to laugh at Calvin's sermons, it was a crime to argue with Calvin on the street. But to enter into a theological controversy with Calvin might turn out to be a very grave crime."[3] Geneva was hardly heaven on earth, though that was the intent. For example, "an overabundance of dishes at the table, a too-elevated headdress, an excessive display of lace, a proscribed color in dress—all were fair subjects of debate and punishment,"[4] and one never knew when the consistory (the church police) would make a house call. One year saw 400 citizens indicted for moral offenses, and, in 60 years, 150 people accused of heresy were burned at the stake.

Calvin's Christianized society was simply not biblical, substituting law for grace. Not only that, it was inconsistent with Calvinist theology. How was one to "Christianize" those in Geneva who were not among God's elect? Characterized as "totally depraved" and not able to respond righteously because they were not extended "irresistible grace," the "non-elect" could never be the Christian citizens that Calvin demanded.

Kingdom-Dominionism took on a new form in the 1940s in Saskatchewan, Canada. An alleged spiritual revival broke out that spawned the "Manifest Sons of God," or, more commonly, the Latter Rain Movement. The eschatology of this movement shifted from the dispensational view, which is the Rapture of the church followed by seven years of tribulation and ending with Armageddon. The movement promoted a more "positive," even triumphant, scenario, looking for God to pour out His Spirit in a great worldwide revival, which would produce "Manifest Sons of God," a.k.a. Joel's Army. These would be believers, continually filled with the Spirit, who would manifest the same signs and wonders that Jesus did and would judge and conquer the world as they ushered in the 1,000-year reign of Christ.

One of the leaders of the movement has said: "God's people are going to start to exercise rule, and they're going to take dominion over the Power of Satan….As the rod of [God's] strength goes out of Zion, He'll change legislation. He'll chase the devil off the face of God's earth, and God's people...will bring about God's purposes and God's reign."[5] This movement, however, ran into the same problems that plagued Calvin in Geneva. The so-called Manifest Sons of God couldn't live up to godly moral standards in practice, even though strict (read "abusive") measures, known as "shepherding," were applied.

The dominionism of the Latter Rain Movement spread far and wide among Pentecostals and Charismatics. Here are some quotes from men whose names you may recognize:

- Yes, sin, sickness and disease, spiritual death, poverty, and everything else that's of the devil once ruled us. But now, bless God, we rule them—for this is the Day of Dominion! (the late Kenneth Hagin)

- Those in [Joel's] army will have the kind of anointing...[Christ's] kind of power...anyone who wants to harm them must die. (the late John Wimber)[6]

- The manifestation of the Sons of God [are] the "overcomers" who will become perfected and step into immortality in order to establish the Kingdom of God on earth. (George Warnock)

The movement was further promoted by the late Bishop Earl Paulk, who taught that Christ was "held in heaven" until His Body, the church, purified itself and the world. Paulk, however, had problems purifying himself, having had a long history of sexual immoralities and was later convicted of perjury. In the 1980s, under Paulk's leadership, charismatic Kingdom Theology joined forces with Calvinistic Dominionist Theology, also known as Christian Reconstructionism, or Theonomy.

Christian Reconstructionism was popularized by Rousas Rushdoony and his son-in-law, Gary North. Reconstructionists believe that by applying the laws of the Old Testament and the principles of the New Testament, the world will be morally transformed by Christians. This, they claimed, would draw people to Christ. Their eschatology is postmillennial, which means that they expect Christ to return after 1,000 years (viewed by some as a symbolic number, meaning that it could be much longer) of successfully reaping the fruit produced by applying the law.

From the 1980s through the turn of the century, a Reconstructionist group called the Coalition On Revival, or COR, greatly influenced conservative evangelicals to seek to transform the U.S. into a Christian-run nation by using the political process. Although the Reconstructionists and the charismatic Kingdom-Now proponents were far apart theologically, the dominionist beliefs that are basic to both camps drew them together. Gary North noted that this surprising liaison made sense in another way: "...bringing together the postmillennial Christian reconstructionists and the 'positive confession' charismatics, with the former providing the footnotes, theology, and political action skills, and the latter providing the money, the audience, and the satellite technology [e.g., TBN and Christian Broadcasting Network]."[7]

A number of years ago, a friend of mine sat in on a meeting of Reconstructionists and asked if they truly intended to apply the biblical laws such as stoning and other capital punishments, to which a national leader of the movement replied, "Absolutely!" It seems that the Calvinist Reconstructionists learned little from the failure of Calvin's totalitarian experiment in Geneva.

The Kingdom-Dominionist movement continues, especially among charismatics, to our present day. Jack Hayford, George Otis Jr., and C. Peter Wagner promoted a form of Kingdom Theology that involved taking back the dominion that Adam and Eve lost in the Garden of Eden. One of the movement's leaders explains, "Jesus gave us His authority and... we are supposed to reclaim, restore, organize, and rule over the earth—not only in a spiritual sense, but through economical, political, educational, and social reform as well." Here is why, this same person tells us, Christians must put to use their God-ordained authority: "Jesus is held in the heavenlies until all things are restored under His feet. He will not and cannot physically return to earth until the church [has brought] a measure of God's ruling authority back to this earth."[8]

This form of Kingdom-Dominionism is rife with methods, rituals, and techniques to be followed in order to seize control. C. Peter Wagner's books *Breaking Strongholds In Your City and Confronting the Powers* contain what he calls "state-of-the-art spiritual methodologies" for taking dominion: identifying territorial spirits, prayer journeys, spiritual mapping, strategic level spiritual warfare, identificational repentance, reconciliation walking, city transformation, praise marches, redeeming the culture, taking our cities, workplaces, and schools for Christ, etc.

I personally experienced the implementation of these techniques during the heyday of Wagner's "strategic level spiritual warfare" influence when some students attempted to "take our local high school for Christ." They buried crosses on the football field and anointed the school windows with oil. Not only did they not take their school for Christ, but they almost caused every Christian student organization to be thrown off campus.

C. Peter Wagner is the chief of operations behind this, and the methods that he says God has given to him are seemingly endless. He is the one who brought John Wimber to Fuller Theological Seminary (FTS) to teach "Signs, Wonders, and Church Growth," later renamed "The Miraculous and Church Growth," which Wagner co-authored with him. Wagner was also the academic mentor who supervised Rick Warren's doctorate dissertation at FTS.

Jack Hayford spent years meeting with Lloyd Ogilvie and other local pastors at Hollywood Presbyterian Church as they applied various spiritual techniques to "transform Los Angeles for Christ." Hayford candidly admitted the failure years later: "My city's [still] being torn on the inside by gang violence and murder, polluted by homosexuality and pornography on the dark side, and suffocated with pride, self-centered snobbishness and sensuality on the 'show' side…[it's] enough to self-destruct us."[9]

All of these movements from church history hold this in common: they are *earthbound*. Focused on setting up the kingdom of God here on earth prior to or in order to expedite our Lord's return, all have a very serious problem. According to the Scriptures, the next kingdom to come on this earth is the kingdom of the Antichrist, which will last for seven years. True believers in Christ will have no part in that kingdom. They will have been removed from this planet by the Lord Jesus and taken to heaven. This event is called the Rapture (John 14:1-3; Philippians 3:20; 1 Thessalonians 5:9-11; 4:16-18; Hebrews 9:28; 1 Corinthians 15:51-52; Colossians 3:4; 1 Thessalonians 1:10; 1 John 3:2-3; Titus 2:13; 1 Timothy 6:14; Revelation 3:10; 2 Timothy 4:8, Luke 12:35,37,40), which will happen prior to the Great Tribulation period, during which time those who have followed the Antichrist will suffer God's wrath.

As Dave Hunt has noted in *Whatever Happened to Heaven?*: "The great seduction is to turn us from heaven to earth, from the true God to ourselves, from the denial of self to the acceptance, love, and esteem of oneself, from God's truth to Satan's lie. At the heart of this seduction are beliefs that have a deceptively spiritual appeal, but which actually turn us from loving Christ and His appearing to the earthly ambition of taking over society and remaking this world into the paradise that Adam and Eve lost" (p. 308).

Much of what has been presented here are some of the historic seeds of an earthbound dominionism that have been sown in Christianity throughout the last 1,000 years. They have taken root and are thriving in the church in this fledgling twenty-first century.

September 2010
(Originally titled "The Temporal Delusion," part 1)

11

Conformation or Transformation?

Love not the world, neither the things
that are in the world. If any man love the world,
the love of the Father is not in him.... And the world
passeth away, and the lust thereof: but he that doeth
the will of God abideth for ever.

— 1 John 2:15-17 —

This series addresses a troubling trend within Christendom
today. Our concern is that if professing believers in Jesus
Christ are hung up on the temporal aspects of life on earth,
then they are caught up in a delusion at best. They are miss-
ing the heart of what God wants for them, and, at worst, they
could be contributing to the kingdom and religion of the
Antichrist.

As was indicated in chapter 10, this earthbound focus
is not a new condition in the history of the world—or the
church, for that matter. From the tower of Babel on, humanity

has attempted to create a utopia and build a kingdom, either independent of God or, allegedly, in the *name* of God but for its own end. For those who call themselves Christians, there is a simple test to discern whether they have fallen prey to such a delusion: are their thinking and actions consistent with what the Word of God says about the kingdom of God, the Rapture of the church, the prophetic end-time warnings of the Word, the final plight of the world in rebellion, and the eternal destiny of those who love the Lord?

The mark of a true Christian is that he or she conforms to what the Scriptures teach. Those who conform to the goals or agendas of the world, either personally or by participating in organized programs that compromise what the Bible teaches, although they may indeed be believers, are nevertheless drifting away from the faith (Hebrews 2:1). This means that one's temporal fruitfulness in Christ and eternal rewards will be adversely affected—but not one's eternal future with Jesus, which was secured by our Lord's full payment for all our sins.

The Bible doesn't make an esoteric issue or a cryptic mystery of what lies ahead for life on this planet. It simply and clearly informs us as to what has taken place in ancient times and what will take place in the future.

From the time of man's first sin against God in the Garden of Eden to our present day, the effects of that sin spawned a progressive evil among mankind. Early on, in response to the proliferation of wickedness, God destroyed all but eight people in a worldwide flood (Genesis 6). Sin has not abated as it continues to separate man from God. Since the days of Noah and his family and their repopulation of the earth, there have been few instances of collective obedience to God. Even among a people chosen of God to whom He would send His Messiah to save the world from sin's consequences, obedience was only sporadic, concluding initially with the rejection and crucifixion of God's anointed Savior, Jesus Christ.

All of that was known to God before the beginning of time, as well as what He would do for mankind in keeping with His unfathomable love for His created beings. His solution for reconciling man to Himself was first indicated after the fall in the Garden of Eden (Genesis 3:15,21) and then foretold by the prophets throughout the Old Testament. God's Savior would become a man through a virgin birth. He would be the God-Man and a suffering Servant, whose sacrificial death would pay for the sins of mankind. His resurrection from the dead certified that the infinite penalty He suffered for a condemned humanity was acceptable in satisfying God's perfect justice.

In the Book of Acts, after commissioning His disciples to share with the world the good news of His salvation, we read of Christ's ascension from the Mount of Olives to heaven and of His future return to that same place (Acts 1:8-11). Both Old Testament and New Testament prophets tell us about significant events that will take place here on earth prior to the Lord's return—and afterward: the destruction of Jerusalem and the dispersion of the Jewish people (Deuteronomy 28:64; Leviticus 26:33); the re-gathering of the Jews to the land of Israel from their worldwide dispersion (Isaiah 11:11-12; 43:6; Ezekiel 20:33-38; 36:24) the return of Jesus for His bride, the church, and His catching believers up to Himself to take them to the wedding in heaven (John 14:1-3; 1 Thessalonians 4:16-18); the seven years of the Great Tribulation, involving worldwide catastrophes that will follow the Rapture of the saints (Jeremiah 30:7; Matthew 24:21-22); the Antichrist's rise to dictatorial leader of the world (2 Thessalonians 2:3-4; Revelation 13); the pouring out of God's wrath upon the earth during the seven years of tribulation (Revelation 6-19); the nations of the world turning against Israel to destroy it (Joel 3:1-2,9-15; Ezekiel 38); the return of Jesus from heaven with His saints, and the destruction of those who have sought to annihilate Israel (Zechariah 12); Jesus' setting up of His throne in Jerusalem and ruling the earth from there for 1,000 years (Revelation 20; Isaiah 65:17-25), and the healing of the earth from the devastation that took place during the Great Tribulation (Isaiah 11:1-10; Ezekiel 47:1-12). At the close of the Millennial reign of Jesus, He will put down a worldwide rebellion led by Satan (Revelation 20:7-9). All those who have rebelled will be cast into the Lake of Fire (Revelation 19:20; 20:10,14-15; 21:8). The heavens and the earth will dissolve, and God will form, in perfection, new heavens, a new earth, and a new Jerusalem for those who love Him, and where righteousness dwells (2 Peter 3:7,10-13).

Just as all the prophecies related to the first coming of Jesus were fulfilled in the smallest detail and with 100 percent accuracy, we can be absolutely sure that the biblical prophecies regarding the future will be just as accurate. Furthermore, they spell out spiritual and physical conditions that will take place. One thing that should be obvious from the prophetic scenario above: this world has a temporal purpose that is incredibly brief compared to eternity. To miss that is to lose sight of the fact that a believer is a "sojourner" here whose "[citizenship] is in heaven; from whence also we look for the Saviour, the Lord Jesus Christ" (Philippians 3:20).

Our responsibility then, as Bereans (Acts 17:11), is to search the Scriptures and compare the movements, programs, agendas, and so forth, that are being promoted today in the world—and especially in Christendom— with what is foretold in God's Word. That will tell us what we may support and what we need to disregard—or even stand firmly against (Ephesians 5:11)

Certainly the world is all about solving its problems without the God of the Bible. Yet many professing Christians are rushing to remedy the world's troubles in ways that are without the support of Scripture, some even in contradiction to what the Scriptures teach. As we have mentioned, Rick Warren's global P.E.A.C.E. plan is one of many programs and teachings that, for the most part, cannot be reconciled with God's prophetic Word. It is Warren's "50-year plan" to cure global issues such as "pandemic diseases, extreme poverty, illiteracy, corruption, global warming, [and] spiritual emptiness." He claims that his social-works agenda developed from his reading of the Gospels—that Jesus gave him the model that was the antidote to the five biggest problems on the planet. Warren subsequently expanded that model from an exclusive endeavor of Christianity to one requiring the support of *all* religions. The "P" in his P.E.A.C.E. plan originally stood for "Planting Churches" as the key antidote for curing the world's ills. Later, however, before a panel and audience of representatives of the world's religions, he changed the "P" from "Planting Churches" to "Promoting Reconciliation."

Warren announced unequivocally that the universal problems *cannot* be solved "without including people of faith and their religious institutions" [Ibid.]. He told his audience at the World Economic Forum at Davos, Switzerland (1/24/08) that the various houses of worship are needed for distribution centers of resources to help eradicate global problems. His shift, however, to an ecumenical program that includes Islamic mosques, Hindu temples, Jewish synagogues, and other religious establishments as participants in meeting social needs may impress the world, but it is contrary to what God says in His Word. The God of the Bible is an exclusive God: "I am the LORD, and there is none else, and there is no God beside me" (Isaiah 45:5). There is to be no participation with the purveyors of false gods. The Apostle Paul tells us we are not to be "unequally yoked together with unbelievers: for what fellowship hath righteousness with unrighteousness? And what communion hath light with darkness? And what concord hath Christ with Belial? Or what part hath he that believeth with an infidel?" (2 Corinthians 6:14-15).

Rick Warren's "ill-curing" ecumenical agenda is illogical as well as unbiblical. How can his game plan for remedying "spiritual emptiness" work with those who promote a false spirituality? Peter tells us, "Neither is there salvation in any other: for there is none other name [Jesus Christ] under heaven given among men, whereby we must be saved" (Acts 4:12). Jesus himself declared, "I am the way, the truth, and the life: no man cometh unto the Father, but by me" (John 14:6). If there is no other true God but the God revealed in the Bible, and if salvation comes only through Jesus Christ—as the Scriptures declare—then all other gods and all other ways of salvation are false, with no hope for their followers. Yet Warren told his Davos religious audience that he was not concerned about their *motivation* in doing good, "as long as you do good." Tragically, he reinforced the very lie that keeps billions of religious people blinded to the truth and from turning to Jesus Christ: works salvation.

The influence of this fix-the-earth program is staggering. Warren's best-selling *Purpose Driven Life* (30 million copies-plus sold worldwide) introduced his "50-year" global P.E.A.C.E Plan and has been translated into 52 languages. According to his website, more than 500,000 evangelical churches are partnering with him in his unbiblical ecumenical effort.

Although Warren's attempt to solve the world's problems is more than misguided, it's not the only prophecy-denying, earthbound enterprise that's gaining followers today. Remember what Rob Bell wrote in *Velvet Elvis*? "The goal isn't escaping this world but making this world the kind of place God can come to."

Brian McLaren, the most prolific of the emerging church writers, has a low, if not distorted, view of biblical prophecy, as do most of his peers in the Emerging Church Movement. He regards the Book of Revelation as "literature of the oppressed" to inspire "each generation," rather than God's warning of future events and judgments to come upon mankind.

Those future events and judgments are clearly at odds with the agenda of solving the world's problems and turning it into a paradise. McLaren declares: "In this light, [that is, removing the prophetic aspect of the Book of Revelation]

Revelation becomes a powerful book about the kingdom of God here and now, available to all." He believes, as does Rick Warren (who also has a low view of prophecy), that it is necessary for all the religions of the world to work together for the greater good of society: "I think our future will also require us to join humbly and charitably with people of other faiths— Muslim, Hindu, Buddhist, Jewish, secularists, and others—in pursuit of peace, environmental stewardship, and justice for all people, things that matter greatly to the heart of God." That sentiment, although pleasing to the flesh, is far removed from the "heart of God" and His Word.

Restoring or preserving this planet as a rallying cause in the church has far exceeded the biblical principle of stewardship today and has become an *earthbound* mindset. Scripture is quite clear that any *abuse* of what God has provided for mankind is sin. Yet some are using the Bible erroneously to support their unbiblical agendas. Eugene Peterson, in his 10-million-bestselling *The Message* Bible, has no qualms about distorting the Scriptures for "the cause." He translates John 3:17 to say that Jesus "came to help, to put the world right again," rather than "that the world through Him might be saved" (meaning the salvation of *souls*–KJV). He then adds to his own "fix the world" agenda by forcing the ecological Green Movement into the Word of God. He brazenly inserts the adjective "green" to Romans 15:13: "Oh! May the God of green hope fill you up with joy…."

Marketing Bibles is big business today, and where there's a "cause," there's usually an attempt to come up with a Bible that implies that the agenda is supported in Scripture. *The*

Green Bible is just one example. It is presented in conjunction with the Sierra Club, The Humane Society, and the National Council of Churches' Eco-Justice Program. It features an introduction by arch-heretic Archbishop Desmond Tutu and contributions by emergent leader Brian McLaren and theologian N. T. Wright, both of whom preach "redeeming the earth." Sales promotions claim that because the Bible mentions the *earth* twice as often as "heaven" and "love," it "carries a powerful message for the earth." That rationale is both delusionary and deceptive. The "powerful message" of the Bible is the "good news" of what God has accomplished to reconcile man to Himself that we might spend life everlasting with Him. This present earth plays a very minute part in God's eternal plan.

The next chapter will address other promoters of the temporal delusion such as Shane Claiborne, Jim Wallis, and Glenn Beck, as well as *The Hole in Our Gospel*, a very popular book advancing the cause of the social gospel.

Sadly, increasing numbers of believers are attempting to secure their lifeboats to our *Titanic*-like earth for the purpose of redeeming it. Instead, our "agenda" needs to line up with the biblical mandate of evangelist and soul winner John Harper. We are told that he was guided of the Lord to change his passage and sail a week later to America on the *Titanic*, knowing that that was where God wanted to use him. Remembered as "the true hero of the *Titanic*" and "God's minister to the perishing," he ran to and fro on the deck helping those in need, giving up his life jacket to another, and asking all that he encountered to turn to God for salvation through Jesus Christ.

As the huge ship began to slip beneath the icy Atlantic waters, Harper leaped from the deck and began swimming toward everyone within sight, pleading with them to come to Christ.

There is no redemption for this earth—only for its people.

Lord, give us that same love for the perishing that You gave to Your servant John Harper, and, by Your grace, use us according to Your Word.

November 2010 (Originally titled, "The Temporal Delusion," part 2)

THE TEMPORAL DELUSION

*Therefore we ought to give the more earnest heed
to the things which we have heard, lest at any time
we should let them slip [away].*

— HEBREWS 2:1 —

The importance of knowing what the Bible teaches and making sure that our thoughts and actions conform to God's Word is underscored by warnings given throughout the New Testament. Consider 2 Timothy 4:3-5:

> For the time will come when they will not endure
> sound doctrine; but after their own lusts shall they
> heap to themselves teachers, having itching ears;
> and they shall turn away their ears from the truth,
> and shall be turned unto fables. But watch thou
> in all things, endure afflictions, do the work of an
> evangelist, make full proof of thy ministry.

The Apostle Paul's prophetic exhortation speaks of a time when those who profess to be Christians will not "endure sound doctrine." Incredibly, they will actually *refuse* to regard the teachings of Scripture as their authority. They will "turn away their ears from the truth" of the Bible and look to the perspective, opinions, and speculations of men. Not only has the Bible ceased to be their authority, but they are denying its *sufficiency* as well. Has that time come upon us?

Although some teach that we are in the Millennium, that Satan has been bound, Christ is ruling mankind from heaven, and things are getting better and better daily, neither the Scriptures nor experience confirm this Amillennial temporal delusion. There is, however, much evidence to support the belief that we are in the "time" of Paul's warning to the church. These are days of increasing apostasy, a stunning abandonment of "the faith" (Jude).

Over the last two decades, "the Church Growth Movement" has had an enormous influence in leading the evangelical church into apostasy. For centuries, "evangelical" described the conservative part of Christianity that believed the Bible to be inerrant and the sole authority in matters of faith and practice. "Evangelical" Christians regarded the Bible as sufficient in all things that pertain to life and godliness. Though many evangelicals still claim to hold to those beliefs, their numbers are decreasing drastically due to recent trends in Christendom.

The Church Growth Movement (CGM) in particular has been a major catalyst in the demise of biblical faith among evangelicals today. In its attempt to attract non-Christians and nominal Christians to its churches, the CGM has implemented worldly concepts and methods to achieve its goal—primarily by employing *marketing* techniques. Central to this approach has been the development of "seeker-friendly," "seeker-sensitive," or "purpose-driven" churches. We have written about this movement extensively, so we will only address here the devastating effect that it has had on "sound doctrine."

Marketing has its place in the business world. When applied to the church, however, it is terribly destructive to biblical teaching. The obvious problem is that the chief focus of marketing is on the customer, or consumer: he or she must always be pleased with what is being offered. This has caused thousands of "evangelical" churches that have subscribed to the seeker-sensitive approach to filter out those things from the Bible that are offensive to the unsaved people who have been attracted to their churches. From a marketing standpoint, certain teachings found in the Bible (even though they constitute sound doctrine and include conviction of sin—not to mention the gospel itself) may offend the consumer. Thus, they must be disregarded in order to ensure that "the customer" will keep coming back.

The CGM has infected thousands of churches around the world and has contributed greatly to the fulfillment of 2 Timothy 4:3-5. The result is an "evangelical" church that has been weaned away from the Word of God. Such a spiritually anemic condition has created hundreds of thousands of weak and biblically shallow Christians who, like dumb sheep, have been relegated to being spoon-fed by marketing-oriented shepherds. Not only will they not "endure sound doctrine," but they will no longer be capable of discerning biblical truth from error. Moreover, the call to be like the Bereans and search the Scriptures to see if what one is being taught by Christian leaders is biblically true (Acts 17:10-11) has been functionally silenced for multitudes of evangelicals.

The CGM is just one of the religious trends in our day that has caused the church to "slip away" from the Scriptures. The drifting away process itself is Satan's primary strategy of turning humanity away from the Word of God, which he effectively accomplished right from the beginning in his seduction of Eve in the Garden of Eden: "Yea, hath God said…?" Planting seeds of doubt and using deceit are obviously his means, but what is his goal and where is all of this heading?

According to the Scriptures, the world is moving toward a one-world religion headed by Satan's man of lawlessness, the Antichrist (2 Thessalonians 2:3-4). His religion will be an apostate Christianity that will be a great distortion of what the Bible teaches yet will maintain a "positive" Christian veneer. Although the Antichrist will not be revealed nor will his apostate church be officially recognized until after true believers have been removed from the earth in the Rapture (1 Thessalonians 4:16-18), his religion and church have been developing for millennia. It doesn't take great insight to see it taking shape before our eyes.

Ecumenism, which originally meant a process of unifying Christian denominations, aberrant groups, and "Christian" cults, has been expanded today to include "people of faith" (i.e., any and all faiths). This is the chief means of developing a one-world religion and church. Since most biblical doctrines are a stumbling block to ecumenical accord, they are dismissed in the interest of harmony. As indicated above, the prophesied rejection of sound doctrine has paved the way for ecumenical unity. With the doctrine of Christ and of God distorted or negated, God himself has been effectively abandoned: "Whosoever transgresseth, and abideth not in the doctrine of Christ, hath not God. He that abideth in the doctrine of Christ, he hath both the Father and the Son" (2 John 9).

For those who profess to follow Christ, the void left by removing sound biblical doctrine as the discerner of God's instructions has been seductively filled by ways that seem "right unto a man, but the end thereof are the ways of death" (Proverbs 14:12). Death involves separation. In physical death, this means the separation of the soul and spirit from the body. Yet it also refers to the separation of oneself from the truth by turning to man's ways. This condition is rampant in Christendom and has fostered agendas that indeed seem right but will have dire consequences in their advancement of apostasy.

In the past two chapters, we have presented examples from church history of various attempts to set up the Kingdom of God or Christian utopias, or to impose a Christian dominionism upon the earth. The fact that all have failed in fulfilling their unbiblical agenda has not deterred further efforts, which seem to be all the more zealous in our day. What is even more striking about such efforts is how separate movements that claim to be Christian have come together in support of the "fix," "restore," "redeem," "take dominion of," or "solve the problems of" the world prior to the return of Jesus. Some declare that Christ cannot return until His servants (i.e., Christians) have fulfilled the "Great Commission" of restoring and establishing God's Kingdom on the earth.

As we've seen, much of what has been proposed above is taught by widely diverse Christian groups and movements that nevertheless claim to adhere to the Bible: the Latter Rain/ Manifest Sons of God and the Kingdom Dominionism of Pentecostals and Charismatics, the Amillennialism of Roman Catholics and Lutherans, the Reconstructionists and Preterists of Calvinism and Reformed theology, the global P.E.A.C.E agenda and the Green and Environmental movements of neo-evangelicals, and the earth-bound promotions of the Emerging Church movement. Not coincidentally, Mormonism and Jehovah's Witnesses have related eschatological views. What, then, of the liberal and left-leaning "social gospel"-oriented Christians who show little interest in biblical truth but are a very large and vocal part of Christendom? Amazingly, they too fit comfortably into this unbiblical "fix the earth" religious unity.

A recent book that demonstrates this clear connection is titled *The Hole in Our Gospel*, authored by Richard Stearns (Thomas Nelson, pub., 2010), president of World Vision U.S. Bill Hybels's Willow Creek Church purchased 10,000 copies, and churches that are part of the Willow Creek Association have likewise ordered thousands of the books. Five pages of endorsements include Chuck Colson, Kay Warren, Bono, Jim Wallis, Tony Campolo, Max Lucado, Ron Sider, Eugene Peterson, Alec Hill, and Leighton Ford, among others. This volume is sprinkled with quotes from Catholic saints and mystics along with Nobel Laureate Mother Teresa (the "poster child" for Stearns's message). An alleged quote from St. Francis of Assisi sets the theme of the book: "Preach the gospel always; when necessary use words" (p. 23).

Stearns's thesis is that Christians have a hole in their gospel if their lives don't demonstrate good works. The "good works" that Stearns has in mind focus mainly on meeting the physical needs of the poor and correcting social injustices throughout the world. Whether or not this is feasible, few could argue with his sincerity—or doubt the nobility of his objective. But is it biblical? From beginning to end, Stearns misuses and abuses Scripture in his attempt to prove his case. For example, he is at the very least confused about the *biblical* gospel. He erroneously speaks of Matthew 25:31-46 as the Final Judgment of the saved and the lost: "Those whose lives were characterized by acts of love done to 'the least of these' were blessed and welcomed by Christ into His Father's kingdom. Those who had failed to respond, whose faith found no expression in compassion to the needy, were banished into eternal fire" (p. 53). Although he attempts to qualify his works-gospel by saying, "This does not mean we are saved by piling up enough good works to satisfy God" (p. 59), he tells us elsewhere that in the example of Lazarus and the rich man, "The plain conclusion is that the rich man went to hell because of his appalling apathy and failure to act in the face of the gross disparity between his wealth and Lazarus's poverty" (p. 187).

The entire tenor of the book reinforces a social gospel that exhorts the reader to work at restoring our planet to righteousness: "Jesus seeks a new world order in which this whole gospel, hallmarked by compassion, justice, and proclamation of the good news, becomes a reality, first in our hearts and minds, and then in the wider world through our influence. This is not to be a far-off and distant kingdom to be experienced only in the afterlife. Christ's vision was of a redeemed world order populated by redeemed people—now" (pp. 243-44). He chides Christians for being "so heavenly minded, you're no earthly good," (p. 2) and adds, "if Jesus was willing to die for this troubled planet, maybe I need to care about it too" (p. 2). Scripture indeed teaches that believers are not to abuse this planet, but that's a far cry from the delusion of trying to renovate it morally and physically through one's "good works." The epistle to the Hebrews, honoring the saints of old as models of faith whom we should emulate, tells us that they saw themselves as "strangers and pilgrims on the earth" and that their desires were for "a better country," i.e., heaven (Hebrews 11:13-16).

Nevertheless, Stearns declares: "The gospel itself was born of God's vision of a changed people, challenging and transforming the prevailing values and practices of our world. Jesus called the resulting new world order the 'kingdom of God'... and said that it would become a reality through the lives and deeds of His followers" (pp. 2-3). In contrast to the title of his book, there is more than a "hole" in the gospel Stearns is fostering. It is clearly "another gospel" (Galatians 1:6-7), a "social revolution" (Stearns's term) that will mislead many and save no one, though it shall bring many together. Stearns quotes Rick Warren: "The first Reformation...was about creeds; this one's going to be about our deeds. The first one divided the church; this time it will unify the church" (p. 51).

This book, even more than Warren's immensely popular *Purpose Driven Life* (which was a platform for solving the world's problems through his Global P.E.A.C.E Plan), will rally professing Christians and the followers of the world's religions, as well as atheists bent on demonstrating their morality sans God—by doing good works. Works-salvation is the faith system for all beliefs but biblical Christianity. Furthermore, the various programs promoting such a faith and practice are gaining the respect and financial support of the world—as long as it accommodates the social welfare of the masses without proselytizing.

According to the Scriptures, there is something terribly wrong when the world is championing the church and its programs. We have seen examples of this throughout the centuries regarding ministries that had wonderful beginnings but now have drifted away from the faith. When was the last time you were exposed to anything remotely Christian at the Y.M.C.A. (Young Men's Christian Association)? When did you last receive a *gospel tract* from that Salvation Army "bell-ringer" at the shopping mall? Moreover, try to find the gospel or an exhortation to directly share the gospel in World Vision U.S.'s mission statement. It's simply not there—by design. These organizations have all succumbed to temporal delusions.

These delusions are manifested when the ways of man are implemented in order to satisfy physical needs at the expense of what God desires for us for eternity. Nothing is to take precedence over the proclamation of the biblical gospel, for it is not just mankind's only hope but his *eternal* hope. Any approach to presenting the gospel that does not clearly and directly reflect the Bible's true content will be a perversion of it, no matter how right or practical it may seem. Any person who participates in programs, practices, or beliefs that dismiss prophetic warnings of the Word of God regarding Last Days events may well become an unwitting contributor to the apostate religion of the Antichrist.

Jesus gives the antidote and the preventive measure that will protect a believer from being influenced and "taken captive" (2 Timothy 2:26) by an increasing number of temporally oriented trends and movements today: "If ye continue in my word, then are ye my disciples indeed; And ye shall know the truth, and the truth shall make you free" (John 8:31-32).

January 2011 (Originally titled "The Temporal Delusion," part 3)

13

APOSTASY AND ITS ANTIDOTE

For we have not followed cunningly devised fables,
when we made known unto you the power and coming
of our Lord Jesus Christ, but were eyewitnesses of his
majesty. . . . We have also a more sure word of prophecy;
whereunto ye do well that ye take heed, as unto a light
that shineth in a dark place. . . .

— 2 PETER 1:16, 19A —

Apostasy is the desertion of one's faith or religion. It is the *forsaking* of the belief to which one had previously adhered. In Acts 21:21 the Apostle Paul is falsely accused of encouraging the Jews to "forsake" the teachings of Moses. The Greek term that is translated "forsake" is *apostasia*. Apostasy, however, rarely comes about abruptly. It is more often a process, and some may contribute to it without becoming complete apostates.

It began in the Garden of Eden. Adam and Eve were in a perfect environment and in perfect fellowship with God. They submitted to God in all things—until, that is, Eve got into a dialog with God's adversary, Satan, the first apostate (see also Isaiah 14:12-14). He had her reconsidering God's Word by questioning what He commanded: "Yea, hath God said...?" The Serpent's objective was to get her to "forsake" the commandment God had given to Adam: they were not to eat of the tree of the knowledge of good and evil (Genesis 2:17; 3:1). Eve succumbed to the seduction, Adam joined his spouse in rebellion against God, and the seeds of apostasy took root.

The seed of apostasy sprouted in Cain, who forsook God's instructions for bringing an acceptable sacrifice and instituted his own type of offering. Apostasy increased with the building of the city and the tower of Babel. It unified people to the degree that God had to "confound the language of all the earth: and from thence did the Lord scatter them abroad upon the face of all the earth" (Genesis 11:9). Later, among the Israelites, Aaron participated in apostasy when he assisted them in their idolatrous worship of the golden calf (Exodus 32).

Throughout the history of the northern and southern kingdoms of Israel many of the kings became apostate. King Ahaz of Judah was a prime example. William MacDonald suggests in his commentary that the prefix of Ahaz's name, "Jeho," which stands for the name of Jehovah God in "Jehoahaz," may have been omitted by the Holy Spirit "because Ahaz was an apostate" (*Believer's Bible Commentary*, pp. 409-10). He endorsed idolatry in Judah and had his son pass through the fire in a ritual to the god Molech. Submitting to Ahaz's instructions, Urijah the priest (who is nevertheless commended in Isaiah) participated in the apostasy by carrying out the king's command to make a copy of a pagan altar and set it up for divination purposes.

APOSTASY AND ITS ANTIDOTE

Ahaz then had the altar incorporated in the Temple worship in Jerusalem.

Apostasy has been a part of every generation since the fall of mankind. Scripture tells us that it will culminate in the last days when the Antichrist is revealed. His religion will be an apostate Christianity—the total antithesis of biblical Christianity. It will accommodate all religions. Although the apostasy will not be fully realized until after the Rapture of the church, its development has been ongoing from the time when sin entered the human race. Furthermore, down through biblical and church history, many true believers, either in ignorance or because of the weaknesses of their flesh, have contributed to apostasy. Solomon seems to exemplify this. As a believer, he was used of the Holy Spirit to build the Temple and to write much of the Book of Proverbs, Song of Songs, and Ecclesiastes, yet he also married many pagan women, which was contrary to Scripture. These women turned him to idolatry and he built temples for them to worship their false gods.

In church history, men such as Augustine and Martin Luther are regarded as true believers, especially by those who hold to Reformation theology. Yet Augustine conceptualized many of the dogmas that are foundational to the false theology and false gospel of the largest apostate institution in Christendom—the Roman Catholic Church. Luther is to be commended for his heroic stance against the Church of Rome but certainly not for his replacement theology and his anti-biblical hatred of the Jews. Later church history is replete with professing and confessing Christians who (knowingly or unknowingly) participated in the development of apostasy.

In summary of the above, apostasy began with the sin of mankind, will greatly increase in the Last Days, and will be complete when the Antichrist rules this earth during the seven-year Great Tribulation period. Therefore, as the world moves toward the apostasy's total fulfillment, *all Christians* will be vulnerable to its destructive seduction.

What is the antidote? How can we keep ourselves from succumbing to those things that would draw us into the apostasy? Let's start with the prevention program presented in Psalm 1: *Blessed is the man that walketh not in the counsel of the ungodly, nor standeth in the way of sinners, nor sitteth in the seat of the scornful.*

The psalmist gives instructions for a spiritually fruitful life in the Lord. These instructions are centered upon our being strengthened by God's Word and begin with the admonition that we are not to follow the counsel of the ungodly. This doesn't mean avoiding counsel only from those who are obviously evil but rather rejecting *any counsel* that does not conform to what is taught in the Word of God. Twice we find in Proverbs (14:12; 16:25) that there is a way that seems right to people but it is not God's way. If it is not God's way, it leads to the ways of death, which means a separation from God's truth that will ultimately lead to destruction in one's life.

A major factor related to the apostasy's subversion of the evangelical church is that fewer and fewer professing Christians really believe in the *sufficiency* of the Word of God for "all things that pertain to life and godliness" (2 Peter 1:3). Instead, evangelicals are turning more and more to the ungodly wisdom of the world. The evangelical church is one of the

✓ Psychology debunked

leading referral entities for psychological counseling services. The shepherds are turning their flocks over to professional psychotherapists, who are, in a sense, the biblical equivalent of hirelings. In addition, they are attempting to increase the numbers of their flocks by turning to marketing techniques, which the Church Growth Movement gleaned from the world. These have proven deadly to biblical faith.

Amen

Scripture's warning against walking in the counsel of the ungodly, standing in the path of sinners, or sitting in the seat of the scornful reveals a progression, which is actually a *regression*—from waywardness to wickedness. By listening to and heeding what the lost—and even the enemies of the faith—have to say, one settles in comfortably with *their* perspective and eventually practices what they preach. The tragic result is that the heart becomes hardened to God's truth, and one's attitude turns to scorn when confronted with it.

The psalmist then shifts from what believers need to avoid to the primary preventative measure they need to incorporate into their lives: *"...his delight is in the law of the Lord* [meaning the Law, the Prophets, and the Testimony], *and in his law* [the Scriptures] doth *he meditate day and night"* (Psalm 1:2).

The main reason that apostasy is spreading so quickly among evangelicals today is that many are functionally biblically illiterate. This means that although nearly all "Christians" have Bibles and are able to read, too few *do* read them, and those who do don't make it a practice that guides their lives. This is one of the reasons for a shocking response revealed by the Pew Forum on Religion & Public Life. It published a survey of more than 35,000 American adults and found that

57 percent of those who claim to be evangelicals believe that "many religions can lead to eternal life."

Obviously, they were not aware of nor did they take seriously the verses in which Jesus declared, "*I am the way, the truth, and the life: no man cometh unto the Father, but by me*" (John 14:6) and Peter exclaimed, "*Neither is there salvation in any other: for there is none other name under heaven given among men, whereby we must be saved*" (Acts 4:12). Scripture tells us that such a condition will be pervasive in the last days: "*For the time will come when they will not endure sound doctrine; but after their own lusts shall they heap to themselves teachers, having itching ears; And they shall turn away their ears from the truth, and shall be turned unto fables*" (2 Timothy 4:3-4).

In our day, biblical absolutes and an exclusive way of salvation are viewed by the world as the epitome of intolerance, an accusation that many evangelicals can't handle—especially those who don't know the Bible well enough to give a biblical response. Meditating upon the Word continually is the obvious solution to rectifying such a condition. Furthermore, there is both encouragement and help from our Lord. Consider His prayer to the Father for believers: "*Sanctify them through thy truth: thy Word is truth*" (John 17:17). Jesus wants us sanctified, or set apart, as those who, regardless of what the world thinks and says, are confident that His Word is the truth. He said, "*If ye continue in my word, then are ye my disciples indeed; and ye shall know the truth, and the truth shall make you free*" (John 8:31-32). Part of that freedom is a confidence to "*earnestly contend for the faith which was once delivered unto the saints*" (Jude 1:3). One cannot "contend" for something of which he is mostly ignorant. Being able to defend one's faith can only come about through a disciplined study of the Scriptures.

In the Book of Proverbs we're told, "*Wisdom is the principal thing; therefore get wisdom: and with all thy getting get understanding*" (Proverbs 4:7). God has made His wisdom available to us in His Word. Furthermore, to all who have put their faith in Jesus, He has given the Holy Spirit, the Spirit of Truth, to help us to "get understanding." Knowing the Holy Scriptures is God's prevention program against apostasy, and it is available to all who seek after Him. That is the biblical criteria for getting wisdom and understanding. The Apostle Paul wrote to Timothy, "*From a child thou hast known the holy scriptures, which are able to make thee wise unto salvation through faith which is in Christ Jesus*" (2 Timothy 3:15). Clearly, it is not a matter of one's intellectual ability or education but rather one's desire to know God's truth and to diligently pursue it. The Lord's choice of uneducated fishermen as apostles to be the primary messengers of His Word—rather than those highly educated within the religious establishment—should speak volumes to anyone who thinks he doesn't qualify.

The believer who meditates continually on God's Word will find that his efforts will be both preventive against apostasy and for the strengthening of his faith. Furthermore, it is the basis for being spiritually fruitful: "*He shall be like a tree planted by the rivers of water, that bringeth forth his fruit in his season; his leaf also shall not wither; and whatsoever he doeth shall prosper*" (Psalm 1:3). It is also the means for equipping the believer for the spiritual war that is now raging.

The crux of the spiritual battle is over the Word of God. The adversary's strategy is to discredit the Scriptures in every way and by every means possible. As we noted, it began in the Garden initially by the questioning of God's Word, followed immediately by the denial of its truth (Genesis 3:4-5). Those who do not recognize that they are in such a battle may have already been captured by the lies of the Adversary. The Apostle Paul wrote that we are not to be ignorant of his devices (2 Corinthians 2:11) and used military metaphors for more than a literary device; he underscored the reality of the spiritual warfare taking place and sets up the believer's defense:

> *Wherefore take unto you the whole armour of God, that ye may be able to withstand in the evil day, and having done all, to stand. Stand therefore, having your loins girt about with truth, and having on the breastplate of righteousness; And your feet shod with the preparation of the gospel of peace; Above all, taking the shield of faith, wherewith ye shall be able to quench all the fiery darts of the wicked. And take the helmet of salvation, and the sword of the Spirit, which is the word of God.* (Ephesians 6:13-17)

Our fight is the good fight of faith, remembering that our weapons are not carnal but spiritual (2 Corinthians 10:4). It is "warfare" over the truth, with the goal of being "able to withstand in the evil day." Our victory is simply to *stand* for God's Word.

As the battle intensifies, which Scripture indicates it will prior to the Lord's coming for His saints, we need to be "*praying always with all prayer and supplication in the Spirit, and watching thereunto with all perseverance and supplication for all saints*" (Ephesians 6:18). We need to circle the wagons with other believers for fellowship and spiritual protection, for counsel, for encouragement, for correction, for comfort, and for ministry to one another. If such things become our practice while we wait upon the Lord, even though the Apostasy dries up the spiritual environment around us, we shall be like a tree planted by the rivers of water, that brings forth its fruit in its season, whose leaf also shall not wither; and whatever we do shall prosper in the Lord.

February 2011

14

READY FOR THE WEDDING?

*Let your loins be girded about, and your lights burning
. . . like unto men that wait for their lord, when he will
return from the wedding; that when he cometh and
knocketh, they may open unto him immediately.
Blessed are those servants, whom the lord when he
cometh shall find watching. . . .*

— LUKE 12:35-37A —

The disciples were greatly troubled as they sat and listened to Jesus say that He was leaving them and that they could not follow Him for a period of time: "Whither I go, thou canst not follow me now; but thou shalt follow me afterwards" (John 13:36). He was going to the Cross. They would also be going the way of the cross, but not just then. He would pay the penalty for their sins and ours. They would later proclaim to the world that Jesus fulfilled divine justice, thereby making the way for mankind to be reconciled to God.

The disciples did not understand the words of Jesus beyond being saddened by them. But then He said something that should have caused them to rejoice: "Let not your heart be troubled: ye believe in God, believe also in me. In my Father's house are many mansions: if it were not so, I would have told you. I go to prepare a place for you....I will come again, and receive you unto myself; that where I am, there ye may be also" (John 14:1-3).

Jesus was speaking to them in terms that were comforting but at the same time perplexing. Though the Gentile mind may not grasp it, His words pictured a wedding that would take place. His part was that of the Groom; their part would be that of the bride. As it was with most of what Jesus had taught them in their short number of years together, they missed the significance. That would all change, however. Following His departure, the Holy Spirit would take up residence within them and give them understanding. "These things have I spoken unto you, being yet present with you. But the Comforter, which is the Holy Ghost, whom the Father will send in my name, he shall teach you all things, and bring all things to your remembrance, whatsoever I have said unto you" (John 14:25-26). Better yet, and amazingly so, their relationship with Jesus would be far more personal and intimate than when He walked with them. The Holy Spirit would indeed bring to their "remembrance" Jesus' words pointing to a future wedding, and the disciples' increasing love for Him would echo a bride's desire to be with her husband-to-be. In other words, the disciples would embrace the reality that they are *the bride* of Christ.

Since true believers in Jesus are disciples of the original disciples, what Jesus had to say to them in John 14:1-3 certainly applies to those of us who have likewise believed upon Him. We are the bride. He has prepared a place for us in heaven. One day, he will return for His bride. In the custom of the ancient Jewish wedding, when the groom left the bride to prepare a place for her in his father's house, she went about making her own preparations for the wedding and her life with her husband-to-be. There's little doubt that her excitement increased as the day of his return drew near. What, then, about "*we*, the bride"? Are we increasing daily in our excitement as we anticipate the coming of our Lord, our Savior, our Groom, our Blessed Hope? If not, there is something terribly wrong. What might put that excitement off?

Perhaps some are only infatuated with Jesus. Although they call themselves Christians, He's like spiritual eye candy that they find attractive in vague "spiritual" ways—but there are too many specific things about Him that they don't care for. Submission is at the top of their "can't take Him too seriously" list. Jesus did, after all, pose the question, "And why call ye me, Lord, Lord, and do not the things which I say?" (Luke 6:46). Their commitment may never have involved giving their heart fully to Him through belief in His death, burial, and resurrection as the only One who could pay the complete penalty for their sins. They were never born again, a criterion Jesus said was necessary for entering the kingdom of God (John 3:3). There is neither an engagement nor a wedding for such folks, nor could there be.

As for those who are truly saved by faith, their affections for Him may have been hindered or cooled down by two common obstacles: their love of themselves and their love of the world.

That won't prevent the wedding, but it plays havoc with the bride's preparation. Preparation? Some don't seem to be aware that every believer is going through a preparation of readiness for the day when he or she will see the Lord. The preparation time involves a myriad of things related to our growth in love for Jesus: sanctification, i.e., truly being set apart for Him; growth in our desire to obey and please Him; thankfulness for His choosing us; increasing fruitfulness in our lives, and joyfulness and excitement in our expectation of seeing Him. The Word of God is filled with the bride's preparation instructions. Sadly, the interest in reading and applying what the manual says is on the wane for many of the betrothed.

Critics of the biblical doctrine of Christ's return for His bride characterize it as a false teaching that encourages an escapist mentality—a kind of "get-your-ticket-and-lounge-around-the-airport" way of thinking, waiting for the "flight to heaven." There are certainly those who think and act that way, supporting the critics' accusations. Although some may cite instances among believers, neither they nor those whom they give as examples have understood the clear teaching of Scripture. John, the beloved of Jesus, gives the bridal preparation instructions: "…abide in him; that, when he shall appear, we may have confidence, and not be ashamed before him at his coming" (1 John 2:28). Moreover, John seems to exude a bride's excitement for seeing Jesus and pleasing Him as he declared, "… we know that, when he shall appear, we shall be like him; for we shall see him as he is. And every man that hath this hope in him purifieth himself, even as he is pure" (1 John 3:2-3). The Apostle Paul says as much in his epistle of encouragement to Timothy:

"But thou, O man of God, flee [sinful] things; and follow after righteousness, godliness, faith, love, patience, meekness. Fight the good fight of faith, lay hold on eternal life, whereunto thou art also called, and hast professed a good profession before many witnesses. I give thee charge in the sight of God…that thou keep this commandment without spot, unrebukeable, until the appearing of our Lord Jesus Christ" (1 Timothy 6:11-14).

Too often, when we are *commanded* to do something, our flesh may react in a way that robs us of the joy that should be involved in obedience; or perhaps we will be deterred from being joyful in our thinking, which then plays out in our lives. That could make for an unenthusiastic bride, at the very least. Yet Jesus said, "If ye love me, keep my commandments….He that hath my commandments, and keepeth them, he it is that loveth me: and he that loveth me shall be loved of my Father, and I will love him, and will manifest myself to him" (John 14:15,21). Furthermore, an erroneous view of what God wants us to do obscures what He has made available to us through our life in Christ. *Nothing* should rob us of our joy in serving the Lord. Peter makes that quite clear: "Wherein ye greatly rejoice, though now for a season, if need be, ye are in heaviness through manifold temptations: That the trial of your faith, being much more precious than of gold that perisheth, though it be tried with fire, might be found unto praise and honour and glory *at the appearing of Jesus Christ*: Whom having not seen, ye love; in whom, though now ye see him not, yet believing, ye *rejoice with joy unspeakable* and full of glory: Receiving the end of your faith, even the salvation of your souls" (1 Peter 1:6-9).

Each of us needs to answer this vital question regarding

our own bridal preparation: How much of it involves rejoic-
ing "with joy unspeakable"? Is that our experience more often
than not? Any lack thereof is no fault of the Lord: "I am come
that they might have life, and that they might have it more
abundantly" (John 10:10). There is no task, no circumstance, no
condition, no problem, no event, no person (other than ourselves!) that can rob us of the joy we have in Christ, especially
when we remember that "neither death, nor life, nor angels,
nor principalities, nor powers, nor things present, nor things
to come...shall be able to separate us from the love of God,
which is in Christ Jesus our Lord (Romans 8:38-39). Then we can
joyfully fulfill the preparatory works "which God hath before
ordained that we should walk in them" (Ephesians 2:10).

 "But Tom, you have no idea what I'm going through!"
That's true, but neither am I oblivious to such things in my
own life, as well as the toll of problems in our world, which
is still reeling under the curse of sin. Nevertheless, through
it all God has made a way for us to "Rejoice, and be exceed-
ing glad: for great is your reward in heaven: for so persecuted
they the prophets which were before you" (Matthew 5:12). Was
Paul conning the Corinthians when he wrote, "I am exceed-
ing joyful in all our tribulation" (2 Corinthians 7:4)? Hardly! He
further encourages us with his prayer and exhortation to the
Colossians: "For this cause we also, since the day we heard it,
do not cease to pray for you, and to desire that ye might be
filled with the knowledge of his will in all wisdom and spiritual
understanding; That ye might walk worthy of the Lord unto
all pleasing, being fruitful in every good work, and increasing in the knowledge of God; Strengthened with all might,

according to his glorious power, unto all patience and longsuffering with joyfulness" (1:9-11). That prayer is God's promise. It may not always be our *experience*, but it is God's Word and His Truth: "Heaven and earth shall pass away, but my words shall not pass away" (Matthew 24:35; Mark 13:31; Luke 21:33).

Dave Hunt writes:

> Ours is a "heavenly calling" (Hebrews 1:3). We have been "blessed with all spiritual blessings in the heavenly places in Christ" (Ephesians 1:3); and it is in heaven that God has reserved for us "an inheritance, incorruptible, and undefiled and that fadeth not away" (1 Peter 1:4). Indeed, our hope is in heaven (Colossians 1:5) where our names have been written (Luke 10:20). No wonder, then, that our resurrection bodies are "spiritual" (1 Corinthians 15:44) and "heavenly" (v. 49; 2 Corinthians 5:2), suited for living in God's presence.
>
> The joy in heaven will be so great eternally that we will need new and glorious bodies to appreciate and express it. Heaven is often thought of as a solemn place of pomp and protocol. We forget what David knew: "In thy presence there is fulness of joy; and at thy right hand are pleasures for evermore" (Psalm 16:11).
>
> Christ endured the cross "for the joy set before him" (Hebrews 12:2), a joy He wanted to share with us in heaven. [Dave Hunt, *When Will Jesus Come?*, Harvest House, 1993]

Growing up Roman Catholic, which involved a continuous and somewhat extensive Catholic education, I was never taught that I was the "bride of Christ"; that was reserved for the nuns. Neither was I taught that Jesus was coming back to take me to heaven. Those who were brought up in churches that strongly adhere to the teachings of the Reformation would most likely be just as uninformed as I was and perhaps even opposed to the doctrine of Christ returning to catch His bride away to heaven. Although the Reformers rejected the false gospel of Rome, they kept some of its baggage, such as infant baptism and particularly its eschatological teaching of amillenialism, which practically dismisses the return of Jesus for His bride. The sad irony here is that the cry of the Reformation was *sola Scriptura*, meaning that the Bible is the believer's *only* authority on matters of faith and practice.

Does the Bible indeed teach the return of Jesus to catch away His bride in order to take her to heaven for the wedding and the feast that He has prepared? Or, as the critics charge, is that the delusion promoted by a 19th century anglo-Irishman named John Nelson Darby? Darby claims that the teaching came from Scripture. The critics and the mockers of this teaching, even in our day, say no. Darby aside (although I believe we owe him a great deal of thanks for encouraging the church to seek out what the Scriptures tell us about this matter), as Bereans, let us "search the Scriptures" to see if these things be so.

As we began this article, Jesus was declaring to His disciples that He was going away to prepare a place for them and said that He would return. The metaphorical context clearly implied a wedding. How might that take place? "Behold, I show you a mystery; We shall not all sleep, but we shall all be changed, In a moment, in the twinkling of an eye, at the last trump: for the trumpet shall sound, and the dead shall be raised incorruptible, and we shall be changed" (1 Corinthians 15:51-52). "For the Lord himself shall descend from heaven with a shout, with the voice of the archangel, and with the trump of God: and the dead in Christ shall rise first: Then we which are alive and remain shall be caught up together with them in the clouds, to meet the Lord in the air: and so shall we ever be with the Lord. Wherefore comfort one another with these words" (1 Thessalonians 4:16-18).

Are these words a comfort to you? I hope so, because that is our "blessed hope," the eternal reality of "ever be[ing] with the Lord"! Or are you distracted by focusing on an earth-bound temporal delusion that is causing you to miss the sublime truth that your eternal citizenship "is in heaven; from whence also we look for the Saviour, the Lord Jesus Christ" (Philippians 3:20)? Our prayer is that we all might be that bride who looks excitedly, expectantly, "for that blessed hope, and the glorious appearing of the great God and our Saviour Jesus Christ" (Titus 2:13). We need to heed the words of our wonderful Groom: "Let your loins be girded about, and your lights burning; And ye yourselves like unto men that wait for their lord....Blessed are those servants, whom the lord when he cometh shall find watching....*Be ye therefore ready* also: for the Son of man cometh at an hour when ye think not" (Luke 12:35-37,40).

15

SEDUCTION:
A PRIMER FOR PERSECUTION?

*Yea, and all that will live godly in Christ Jesus
shall suffer persecution.*

— 2 TIMOTHY 3:12 —

For the last three decades, Dave Hunt and I have addressed many trends and teachings that have influenced the evangelical church, particularly in the United States. Our concern has focused primarily on unbiblical beliefs and practices that were turning Christians away from the Word of God. Twenty-five years ago, we wrote *The Seduction of Christianity*, a rather controversial book that was motivated by feedback from those who had read Dave's earlier books and had watched the film documentaries to which I had contributed in the early eighties. Some dealt specifically with religious cults (*Cult Explosion*, *The God Makers*, etc.). Responses from Christians who read those books and watched the films, however, alerted us to the fact that the cult beliefs that we identified were also being taught in their churches, which were being influenced by leading

Charismatic and Word/Faith teachers. Those same false teachers were also spreading cultish doctrines throughout the country on Christian television networks.

One of the principal false teachings at the time was the belief that godhood could be attained by created beings. Though that is foundational to Mormonism ("As man is, God once was; as God is, man may become") and Hinduism (self-realization is realizing that man is God), it had worked its way in various forms and methods into different "Christian" movements, teachings, and practices. Much of it was promoted by extreme Charismatics, but it was also finding its way into conservative evangelical churches through so-called Christian psychology (with its emphasis on self and self-esteem, leading to the exaltation and deification of self). Of course, the lie that man could become a god was the cornerstone of Satan's *seduction* of the human race (Genesis 3:1-5).

In his war against those who have committed their lives to the true and living God, Satan, as God's chief adversary throughout history, has majored in *seduction* and *persecution*. Although persecution would seem to be more effective in its prohibition of Christianity than seduction (and it certainly generates more fear), it is far less productive for the Adversary in achieving his objective. The saying that "the blood of the martyrs is the seed of the church" has been demonstrated throughout church history. Martyrdom and other forms of persecution have always increased and/or *strengthened* the body of Christ. The same, however, cannot be said for seduction.

Believers in the United States have never experienced significant corporate religious persecution—certainly nothing like what has taken place in China, India, or throughout countries controlled by Islam. Historically, true Christians in the West as far as Europe have suffered violence from the Caesars of Rome, the Church of Rome, and Communism, among others, but a comparable level of persecution has yet to reach our shores. On the other hand, spiritual seduction has proliferated here and has shipwrecked the faith of many within Christendom.

Unlike persecution, there is not even a remote value associated with seduction; it is spiritually debilitating and deadly. Stories abound of those believers who have survived and been strengthened in their faith during the persecution they suffered in communist countries only to have their walk with the Lord devastated after they escaped to the West. They could endure persecution, but they could not resist seduction.

The thesis of this chapter, which is that seduction will ultimately bring about persecution, is intimidating for me personally. Why? Partly because Dave and I have only rarely addressed the potential for persecution in the U.S. and partly because it's only beginning to show its nasty head here. Then why write about it now? From my observations, increasing signs point to a pending clash between the professing—and even true—Christians who will conform to the world by compromising biblical teachings and those who will remain steadfast in the faith. Nevertheless, I put little value in my observations unless I'm confident that they reflect what the Scriptures teach. Nor should anyone who reads this.

Here are seven pertinent verses (among others that could be given) that have influenced my observations and this thesis:

In Matthew 24:4, Jesus warns that the last days prior to His return will be a time of religious deception: "Take heed that no man deceive you." He adds (v. 24) that the deception will be so great that if it were possible the very elect could be deceived. In Matthew 7:13-14, Jesus refers to the "strait gate" and "narrow way" that leads to life and announces that "few there be that find it." Luke writes (18:8) the sobering words of our Lord regarding the time of His return: "Nevertheless when the Son of man cometh, shall he find faith upon the earth?" Since His Second Coming is for the purpose of judgment and to save Israel from annihilation, His words here seem better suited to His coming for His bride in the midst of a professing Christianity that has joined the apostasy. The Apostle Paul gives this insightful explanation as to how apostasy could manifest among those who call themselves Christians: "For the time will come when they will not endure sound doctrine; but after their own lusts shall they heap to themselves teachers, having itching ears; And they shall turn away their ears from the truth, and shall be turned unto fables" (2 Timothy 4:3-4).

Sound doctrine will not be endured in the last days because many who began with the milk of scriptural truth have already been weaned away from it, i.e., seduced, by their own lusts and by false teachers. More than that, sound doctrine will become an issue that will foster division among Christians. Paul instructed the Roman believers to identify those who teach things "contrary to the doctrine which ye have learned; and avoid them" (Romans 16:17). It's clear that believers who desire to stand firm for the teachings of God's Word will be at odds with Christians whose beliefs and lives are not conformed to the Scriptures.

Could division over doctrine result in persecution? Both history and the Word of God indicate as much. In the Book of Acts, we are told that "there was a great persecution against the church which was at Jerusalem" (Acts 8:1). It involved violent assaults, imprisonments, and deaths, and the issues were doctrinal—pitting those who fiercely defended the religious traditions of men against those who followed the teachings of Jesus the Messiah. Persecutions continued as Christians who stood firm in the doctrine of Christ refused to bow down to the deified Caesars or conform to the pagan rituals of Rome. They became vicious entertainment for those who packed the coliseums to see them burned and torn apart by animals. Later, a "Christianized" Rome persecuted those who attempted to reform Roman Catholicism. From there, doctrinal inquisitions and trials by torture proliferated against the "protestants" and other biblical non-Catholics. Today, persecution continues against believers in Islamic countries and in those places in the West where Roman Catholicism still controls the society, such as cities, villages, and even some states in Mexico and South America.

Although none of the above has manifested itself substantially in the United States, could such religious persecution take place here? Roman Catholicism has never been in a position to impose its dogmas on the American populace; Islam has only begun to control some neighborhoods here with its Sharia legalism ("Terror's Secret Weapon: Shariah," *Townhall*, 4/20/11). But what about a scenario of Bible-believing Christians being persecuted by other Christians who will "not endure sound doctrine"? Is that likely? Some who have previewed this article were doubtful that "Christians killing Christians over doctrines" would ever take place here, a law-abiding country where, for the most part, "doctrinal apathy" rules among evangelicals. I tend to agree, yet if someone had told me 25 years ago that evangelicals would shift from the then highly influential moral

1970's / AlphA / USA

majority/Christian Right to the socialism-oriented Christian Left—I would have laughed. No one is laughing at that reality now. Only the Lord knows how extreme the oppression will become prior to His return for His bride, but there are many forms of persecution, short of martyrdom.

We have already addressed significant trends among evangelicals that have "weaned them off the Word," seducing them into following the ways, means, and agendas of *man* contrary to the Scriptures. In the midst of that process of compromise, increasing numbers of professing and true Christians have accepted the ideals of the world, including moral, social, and religious tolerance. "Intolerance" in thought, word, or deed of that which the world believes is good for humanity identifies a person as antisocial at least and as bigoted, prejudiced, or a practitioner of hate crimes at worst. Furthermore, what if a social gospel that is based upon "good works" became widely accepted as a better form of "salvation"—one that had the potential to rally *everyone* together, including governments, the world's religions, liberal Christians and cults, humanists and even atheists? Everyone, that is, *except biblical Christians*. What might be the consequences for those who would object to such a world-supported "Christian" development because it did not conform to sound doctrine?

Sound doctrine, i.e., the teachings of the Bible, is what a true Christian is to abide by as one lives his life for Christ. Sound doctrine is the *absolute criterion* that dictates what beliefs, practices, and programs he can accept and what he must reject. Moreover, Scripture exhorts him to be discerning and steadfast in its teachings: "Wherefore take unto you the whole armour of God, that ye may be able to withstand in the evil day, and having done all, to stand. Stand therefore, having your loins girt

about with truth, and having on the breastplate of righteousness....And take the helmet of salvation, and the sword of the
Spirit, which is the word of God" (Ephesians 6:13-14,17).

But would God allow persecution to take place *within* the
church? That's what Peter seems to be acknowledging: "For
the time is come that judgment must begin at the house of
God: and if it first begin at us, what shall the end be of them
that obey not the gospel of God?" (1 Peter 4:17). Judgment, in the
sense of correction and strengthening that results from God's
allowing of persecution, as we've noted, has always been a part
of Christianity. The Epistle to the Hebrews also indicates that
persecution is one of the things that God has used as a spiritual
pruning and purifying process for Hebrew Christians.

If you're not sure how (or why) persecution might take
place within Christianity, consider these examples: When
Promise Keepers enjoyed popularity among evangelical men,
it became known that one of its goals was to "break down the
walls" between Catholics and evangelicals. Part of that process
involved turning churches against ministries that evangelized
Roman Catholics. When Rick Warren's "40 Days of Purpose"
began to influence hundreds of thousands of churches throughout the U.S., long-time members who protested on doctrinal
grounds were either disfellowshiped, or threatened with disfellowship, unless they submitted to Warren's program in their
own churches. To question a pastor or the elders' support for
introducing yoga or "Christianized yoga" in a church has been
grounds for disfellowship.

Although the above examples may seem marginal to some,
they and other endeavors, including church-growth marketing
programs, emerging church methods and mystical practices,

ecumenical overtures to Muslims and Mormons, an ecumenical global P.E.A.C.E. plan that involves all the world's religions, movements aimed at solving the world's ecological, poverty, and social injustice problems, etc., have driven multitudes of believers to start home churches.

What if you were to preach against the various agendas mentioned above because they were a rejection of sound doctrine? Remember the Apostle Paul's admonition? "I charge thee therefore before God, and the Lord Jesus Christ...Preach the word; be instant in season, out of season; reprove, rebuke, exhort with all longsuffering and doctrine. For the time will come when they will not endure sound doctrine..." (2 Timothy 4:1-4). What would be the reaction among those within and without the church who were supportive of those agendas?

Or what if even *without* your preaching or protesting it simply becomes known that you are one of those biblical Christians who is intolerant toward other religions, who rejects evolution, who won't go along with psychology, who is anti-abortion, anti-genetic manipulation, and anti-euthanasia; that you view homosexuality as a sin rather than an alternative lifestyle, and that you are against gay rights and gay marriage? Furthermore, you seem to be out of touch with the acceptable morality of the day (marriage now being statistically a minority as a practice in the U.S.) by having a "problem" with cohabitation, and it's been said that you believe sexual abstinence should be practiced outside of marriage. You are suspicious about the alarm over "global warming." It's become known that you support Israel against the alleged right of the Palestinians to be restored to the land they believe is theirs. How will such a person be dealt with in Christendom—as well as by the world that champions everything that a believer opposes? The dark clouds of persecution appear to be gathering over the church in the U.S.; signs indicate that the seats of the "coliseum" are beginning to fill with a widely diverse audience that, at least in a figurative sense, has "a taste for the blood" of those who reject their programs and teachings on the basis of sound biblical doctrine.

The seduction of Christianity has created a condition in which biblical discernment and steadfastness in the faith are the exception rather than the rule. Standing for the truth and righteousness of the Word of God while the opposition increases within and without the church can only result in some form of persecution. Paul makes that quite clear: "*Yea, and all that will live godly in Christ Jesus shall suffer persecution*" (2 Timothy 3:12). Although that verse may distress some believers, it shouldn't. Why? Because the beginning of the verse gives a believer the key to receiving the grace to glorify God and to benefit others through persecution: living godly lives in Christ Jesus! That is a believer's only preparation and it is more than sufficient. Jesus, who is the Word made flesh, gave His disciples this astonishing word of encouragement regarding standing for His teachings: "Blessed are ye, when men shall hate you, and when they shall separate you from their company, and shall reproach you, and cast out your name as evil, for the Son of man's sake. Rejoice ye in that day, and leap for joy: for, behold, your reward is great in heaven…" (Luke 6:22-23). Our prayer is that the Lord Jesus will help us to live godly lives and by His grace remain steadfast in the faith as we look for His soon coming.

ENDNOTES

Chapter 4

1. *Inside the Vatican*, March/April 2004, 24.

2. See T. A. McMahon, *Showtime for the Sheep?* (Bend, OR: The Berean Call, 2004).

3. Tony Campolo, *Letters to a Young Evangelical* (New York, NY: Perseus Books Group, 2006), 20.

4. Tony Jones, *The Sacred Way* (Grand Rapids, MI: Zondervan, 2005), 53.

5. Ibid.

6. Ibid., 92.

Chapter 5

1. Robert E. Webber, *Ancient-Future Faith: Rethinking Evangelicalism for a Postmodern World* (Baker Academic, 1999), 15.

2. Ibid., 17.

3. Mark Galli, "Lost Secrets of the Ancient Church," *Christianity Today*, February 2008, 23.

4. Ibid., 24.

5. http://en.wikipedia.org/wiki/Evangelical_Orthodox_Church.

6. Galli, *Christianity*, 28.

7. Robert Webber, *Signs and Wonders* (Nashville, TN:Star Song Publishing Group, 1992), 5.

8. Peter Gillquist, "Arrowhead Springs To Antioch: Odyssey To Orthodoxy," *The Word*, October 1987.

Chapter 7

1. Romans 1:16.
2. John 10:30-33.
3. 1 Timothy 2:5.
4. John 14:6, John 3:16-17.
5. Isaiah 59:2.
6. 1 John 2:2.

7. Hebrews 10:10-12.
8. Hebrews 12:2.
9. Romans 1:3-4.
10. 2 Corinthians 7:10.
11. Romans 5:6.
12. Ephesians 2:8.
13. John 3:15.
14. Romans 5:18.
15. John 3:3.
16. Galatians 2:20, 1 Peter 1:23.
17. Colossians 1:27.
18. 1 Corinthians 6:19.
19. 2 Timothy 3:16-17.
20. John 16:13.

Chapter 10

1. R. W. Southern, *Western Society and the Church in the Middle Ages* (Penguin Books, Vol. 2 of *Pelican History of the Church Series*, 1970), 18-19, cited in Dave Hunt, *Whatever Happened to Heaven?* (Harvest House, 1988), 150-51.

2. Will Durant, *The Reformation: A History of European Civilizations from Wyclif to Calvin: 1300-1564* (Simon & Schuster, 1957), 472-73, cited in Hunt, *Heaven*, 175-76.

3. Edwin Muir, *John Knox: Portrait of a Calvinist* (The Viking Press, 1929), 106-8, cited in Hunt, *Heaven*, 174-75.

4. Hunt, *Heaven*, 174.

5. Ern Baxter (associate of William Branham), cited in Sandy Simpson, "Dominionism Exposed," http://www.deceptioninthechurch.com/dominionismexposed.html.

6. Referenced in Joel's Army Youth and Young Adult Conference purpose statement, http://www.elijahlist.com/words/display_word/1760.

7. Gary North, *Christian Reconstructionism: The Attack on the "New" Pentecostal,* January/February 1988, Vol. X, No. 1.

8. Dr. Kluane Spake, "Dominion Theology and Kingdom NOW," http://hubpages.com/hub/Dominion-Theology—by-Dr-Kluane-Spake.

9. Jack Hayford, cited in Dr. Peter Wagner, "Let's Take Dominion Now," http://www.intheworkplace.com/apps/articles/default.asp?articlid=22902&columnid=1935.

ABOUT THE BEREAN CALL

The Berean Call (TBC) is a non-denominational, tax-exempt organization which exists to:

ALERT believers in Christ to unbiblical teachings and practices impacting the church

EXHORT believers to give greater heed to biblical discernment and truth regarding teachings and practices being currently promoted in the church

SUPPLY believers with teaching, information, and materials which will encourage the love of God's truth, and assist in the development of biblical discernment

MOBILIZE believers in Christ to action in obedience to the scriptural command to "earnestly contend for the faith" (Jude 3)

IMPACT the church of Jesus Christ with the necessity for trusting the Scriptures as the only rule for faith, practice, and a life pleasing to God

A free monthly newsletter, THE BEREAN CALL, may be received by sending a request to: PO Box 7019, Bend, OR 97708; or by calling

1-800-937-6638

To register for free email updates, to access our digital archives, and to order a variety of additional resource materials online, visit us at:

www.thebereancall.org

BEND • OREGON